A Pastoral Proposal for an Evangelical Theology of Freedom

A Pastoral Proposal for an Evangelical Theology of Freedom

A Respectful Response to the Expressed Hope of Dr. Karl Barth

ALBERT J.D. WALSH

WIPF & STOCK · Eugene, Oregon

A PASTORAL PROPOSAL FOR AN EVANGELICAL THEOLOGY OF FREEDOM
A Respectful Response to the Expressed Hope of Dr. Karl Barth

Copyright © 2013 Albert J.D. Walsh. All rights reserved. Except for brief quotations in critical publications or reviews, no part of this book may be reproduced in any manner without prior written permission from the publisher. Write: Permissions, Wipf and Stock Publishers, 199 W. 8th Ave., Suite 3, Eugene, OR 97401.

Wipf & Stock
An Imprint of Wipf and Stock Publishers
199 W. 8th Ave., Suite 3
Eugene, OR 97401
www.wipfandstock.com

ISBN 13: 978-1-62032-649-7
Manufactured in the U.S.A.

All scripture quotations, unless otherwise indicated, are taken from the Holy Bible, New International Version®, NIV®. Copyright ©1973, 1978, 1984 by Biblica, Inc.™ Used by permission of Zondervan. All rights reserved worldwide.

Unless otherwise noted, all Scripture quotations are taken from the Holman Christian Standard Bible®, Copyright © 1999, 2000, 2002, 2003, 2009 by Holman Bible Publishers. Used by permission. Holman Christian Standard Bible®, Holman CSB®, and HCSB® are federally registered trademarks of Holman Bible Publishers.

To the faculties of Princeton Theological Seminary, Lutheran Theological Seminary of Philadelphia, Moravian Theological Seminary, and Pittsburgh Theological Seminary.

Soli Deo gloria

Contents

Preface ix
Introduction xv

1 The Foundation and Fundamental Problem 1

2 Israel: Dialectic of Obedience-Disobedience 16

3 The New Testament Witness to Graced Freedom 38

4 The Testimony of Paul to Graced Freedom 56

5 The Book of Revelation: Freedom for Humanity 69

6 The Ecumenical Characteristics of Graced Freedom 92

Conclusion: Prospects for Pastoral Ministry 105
Bibliography 115

Preface

IN THE AUDIO VERSION of the lectures given by Dr. Karl Barth when he paid his first and only visit to the United States, lectures that were eventually published under the title *Evangelical Theology*, and in his closing remarks, Karl Barth expressed his hope to see a theology native to North America that would suffer from neither an inferiority complex in relation to good old Europe, nor a superiority complex in relation to Asia and Africa (somewhat prophetic). Karl Barth then expressed his *hope* for the development in the United States of a theology of freedom, and more particularly, a theology of freedom *for* humanity! Whether in fact such a theology has been written in the interim, we do not know; in our own theological reading, study, and research we have yet to encounter such a theological expression. This essay is a proposal, recommending those elements and/or characteristics that could be considered central to the formation of such a theology, and primarily from the perspective of a *pastoral* theologian, and based on the evangelical witness of the apostles, evangelists, and prophets.

We do not intend the italicized word (i.e., *pastoral*) to be in any way pejorative, as if pastoral theology were somehow something less important, less professional, or as possessing less intellectual integrity and rigor than do the more academic forms of theological reflection and explication. The italicization of the word *pastoral* is, instead, meant to affirm the centrality of the context out of which this particular proposal speaks, and to affirm as well how this particular context presents us with some of the more challenging issues to be faced in contemporary Christianity. If theology is fundamentally at the service of the Church catholic and the Church's immense responsibility for the proclamation of the gospel, then this context (i.e., pastoral service), and the wider context of the *ekklēsia* in the world, should be understood as vital to the development of a proposal for and further expansion of a theology of freedom. There can be no genuine comprehension of the "graced freedom" proposed if one considers it to be little more than some abstract principle; this freedom is *for* humanity, and those who embrace such freedom will soon discover that it is an extremely relevant and practical reality, with supremely relevant and practical implications for the life we must live. To deny that this graced freedom has practical implications will also and at the same time diminish the proclamation of the gospel of Jesus Christ, and the reality of redemption and reconciliation in Christ, to little more than an abstract principle; the incarnation assures us that the graced freedom proposed in this essay is a matter of what has been made real in the flesh and *for us* and *for our salvation*.

CLARIFICATION OF TERMS

From the start it is essential to note that we are not talking about liberty, a term that has taken on connotations that are, in my estimation, almost the polar opposite of what can be described as evangelical freedom from the point of view of a theology shaped, as it should be, by the witness of Holy Scripture and the explication of Scripture as handed down to us in the theological traditions of our evangelical faith. Liberty is applicable to the external realities of one's life and impacts accessibility to a certain kind of freedom that will either impair or enlarge one's choices. The Statue of Liberty is representative of this form of freedom, as is so clearly expressed in the poetic words she bears: "Give me your tired, your poor, your huddled masses yearning to breathe free, the wretched refuse of your teeming shores. Send these, the homeless, tempest-tossed to me. I lift my lamp beside the golden door."

Perhaps Dr. Barth was being somewhat tongue in cheek when he suggested that the Statue of Liberty should be made subject to *demythologization*; nevertheless, a theology of freedom would assert that the poetic phrase, engraved on the Statue of Liberty, bears witness to the external nature of the liberty being extended, by way of her lamp, and represents a reality that is different from the freedom being advocated in this essay. Excepting the Constitutional language of *inalienable rights*, aspects of such liberty would include responsibilities of one's citizenship, commitment and obedience to the order of law, regular engagement in the political order, perhaps even the pursuit of happiness, which demonstrate the externality of liberty and its effects. This liberty is, in fact, conferred upon the citizen, and mimetically confessed (that is, to be seen as a secular confessional affirmation) in the Pledge of Allegiance; in confessing allegiance to the flag, the citizen confesses allegiance to *all* the flag represents symbolically.

Preface

Nevertheless, might we who live by the light of that lamp of Liberty not also see the use of such liberty as an opportunity to proclaim that greater freedom, which is evangelical freedom? Stated in more concrete terms, does not the benefit of such liberty provide the *ekklēsia* in the United States with a particular and practical responsibility—for proclaiming the graced freedom *made real* in Christ and enacting, in service to *humanity* and in the name of God and the gospel of God, that same freedom? Is it appropriate (to say the very least) for the *ekklēsia* in the United States to benefit from such liberty, while denying the God-given mandate of the gospel to proclaim, in word and deed, that graced freedom essential to the enrichment of humanity and found in the gift of God in Christ Jesus? One purpose of this essay is to establish the necessity for such as fundamental to the development of an evangelical theology of freedom *for* humanity; recognizing, as we do, that graced freedom is first and properly given in obedience to God, and secondarily given in service to the neighbor (as the concrete expression of the two-fold love of God and neighbor).

Regrettably, for many today, the word liberty has come to be associated with the all-too-limited concept of individual rights and in extreme measure, the privatization of personal choice; so much is this the case that one finds resistance to the mere suggestion that there are boundaries and demands of what can be reasonably expected of a citizen, external to the individual, to which he or she is obligated in order to maintain what could only be called the common welfare of the community at large. Even more evident is a form of relativism that has collapsed all truth claims into a vast sea of generalization, and so one is at liberty to select that claim which he or she feels best expresses his or her individuality. One cannot assert knowledge of the truth in any way whatsoever, as such truth is said to be non-existent, or merely a misguided claim to self-assertion; one can only speak of the truth in general, as all truth claims are said to be relative if not equal in value.

The one showing the greatest tolerance for and acceptance of all truth claims, as having an equal and legitimate claim to a place in the common marketplace of ideas, is thought to be demonstrating the essence of liberty in and through his or her character. None of this is to say that the word liberty has lost all currency or needs to be retrieved from the trash bin of post-modernity; it is rather to suggest that the way in which the concept of liberty is understood in much of contemporary culture and society cannot bear the full weight of meaning located in the concept of graced freedom as proposed in this essay.

Preface

It is not merely the culture or society at large that have been adversely influenced by a limited concept of liberty; the community of faith has now had much of its own self-understanding and substantive ministry shaped and informed by a misconceived application of liberty and its several distorted manifestations (e.g., self-worth as primary; self-assertion; self-enrichment; self-determination; etc.). The vital nature of this essay is found in prior pastoral experience with the manifold ways by which this influence has distorted understanding of the *ekklēsia* as essentially determined by the Spirit of Christ, under the Lordship of Christ as event, and as accountable to Christ and Christ alone. Even more troubling is the manner in which many in the church/Church have come to embrace liberty as the true substance of the gospel; this has led to several critical and unfortunate distortions of Christian doctrine and dogma that are fundamental to orthodox faith and confessional practices. We will take up this same problem in a later chapter of this essay.

Liberty can be, even in its contemporary setting, understood to be a manifestation of what the apostle Paul refers to as *principalities and powers*, in the sense that it is built into the order of creation and structured for the purposes of preserving the dignity and just governance of any one nation of people. This would also imply that, as consequence of the Fall, liberty is often subject to the abuse of those same principalities and powers, to be engaged in ways that are contrary to the intent for which God purposed such liberty, and therefore in conflict with the will of God for its rightful purpose and use.

There was liberty (we are not yet speaking of—graced freedom) in the Garden of Eden (Gen. 1:26–31) in which Adam and Eve could enjoy all the richness of their environment, but within the evident limitations and restrictions (external to them and of God, see Gen. 2:15–17) that had been placed upon them. As we will touch on briefly in a later chapter of this essay, there is also a biblical sense in which a particular form of freedom is the mirror image of liberty as an external reality. We will also need to address the sense in which Adam and Eve were created by God with ontological[1] freedom, forfeiting such graced freedom in the disobedience and rebellion

---

1. In use of the term "ontological," we refer to that which is the fundamental and essential nature of this being as a creature created *imago Dei*, the complete disfigurement of that same nature subsequent to the Fall, and the redemption and restoration of that same essential nature in the God-man Jesus Christ and, subsequently, by virtue of the presence of the Holy Spirit in the life of the believer, evidenced as a "new creation" (in the image of the "New Adam").

Preface

of sin, which led to bondage in a multiplicity of forms to which Scripture also bears witness.

As a tentative and initial expression of the much larger argument that needs to be made in the body of this essay, the concept of graced freedom being proposed is not merely an external reality, but is more accurately understood as an ontological reality with extraordinary manifestations in every aspect of the existence of the freed person. While we contend throughout that there can be no division or separation between what is recognized as an ontological reality and the outward actions that give evidence to the actuality of such graced freedom, we would not want to suggest that such association prohibits treating either in isolation from the other. Rather, it is because the ontological reality of graced freedom is manifest in actions (understood in the widest and fullest sense of *event*) that they must be treated in dialectical fashion; we will say more about this dialectic in the introduction.

Furthermore, in light of the expressed hope of Dr. Barth we will contend that such graced freedom is, at its core, a freedom *for* humanity. This graced freedom is: (1) the foundation of redemption as the re-affirmation and re-actualization (i.e., recapitulation) of genuine *anthropos* (humanity created—*imago Dei*, and as male and female), as a new creation in Christ, in both the individual and larger sense of the term, and under the empowerment and continuing presence of the Holy Spirit; (2) the ground for the establishment of the New Testament *ekklēsia*, the body of Christ, and the collective manifestation of such evangelical freedom; the event in which such freedom is to be received, acknowledged, confessed, and expressed; and (3) the basis for the *missio Dei* and ministry as an expression of graced freedom in the *ekklēsia*, where freedom *for* humanity is evident as a passion for the furtherance of justice, integrity, and the enrichment of humanity in free obedience to Christ Jesus and as mandated by his gospel. In any and every instance, God alone is the Subjective Agent of graced freedom, while humanity is the objective recipient and beneficiary. As objective recipient and beneficiary of graced freedom, the human being and *ekklēsia* together—as *imago Christi*—become the subjective agents of the proclamation of such freedom *for* humanity in, with, and for the world, and as event.

In the introduction, and in other appropriate context throughout this essay, we make extensive use of the Greek term *ekklēsia*[2] rather

---

2. The reader is directed to the article addressing the Greek term *ekklēsia* located in the *Theological Dictionary of the New Testament*, 394–402. The conclusion to this

Preface

than the more familiar use of church/Church under the conviction that *ekklēsia* more adequately conveys the concept of event, as opposed to the implication of institution or localization of denominational presence normally associated with the use of church/Church. However, whenever we make use of the more familiar terms (i.e., church/Church), the intention is exactly to call to mind the more institutionalized and denominationally centered manifestation. This choice of terminology (*ekklēsia*) is directly related to the proposed concept of graced freedom which, like the *ekklēsia* itself, is also and always an event, in that it is the union of ontological reality and consequent actions.

Having some degree of sensitivity for the issues raised these days regarding the need for inclusive language in any reference to humanity (as individual or corporate reality), we find constant reference to either the human, humanity, or human being as incapable of bearing the full measure of what the Bible refers to by way of Man as male and female. Therefore, in both the introduction and in select portions of the essay that follows, we have chosen to make use of the biblical *anthropos*[3] (the biblical-theological term for the human as male and female, which we will use for humanity in general and as part of the created world). We will allow the context to determine the reference to either the individual or the corporate; for example, where *anthropos* refers to the individual it will be followed by he/she, him/her, and where the term applies to humanity in general, it will be followed by "them, they, or their."

We now turn to the introduction for a fuller explication of what will be covered in even greater detail chapter by chapter and to the conclusion of this essay.

---

extensive article is most helpful in illuminating our choice of this term: "The NT itself makes no distinction between an invisible triumphant church and a visible militant church. The church, as the individual congregation representing the whole, is always visible, and its righteousness and holiness are always imputed through faith. Luther recognizes this when he prefers the term 'congregation' to 'church' in his rendering of Scripture. Yet if the ideal is not played off against the reality, no more is the whole church against the local congregation. Every congregation represents the whole church, that at Corinth no less than at Jerusalem. The development of larger organizations does not alter this basic truth" (401–2).

3. See the article in *Theological Dictionary of the New Testament*, 59–60.

Introduction

AS STATED IN BOTH title and preface, this is a pastoral proposal for the development of an evangelical theology of freedom and is, therefore, an expression of pastoral care (traditionally, care of souls) in the mode of a practical theology addressing both the *ekklēsia,* and the wider fields to which the *ekklēsia* is called in service to the one gospel of Jesus Christ, and in free obedience to the command of her Lord (there is no genuine obedience that is not free obedience, as one can only speak of genuine love as freely given). It addresses the *ekklēsia* out of the conviction that before we can speak of those actions endemic to graced freedom in and through her numerous avenues of service in Christ to the world, we must raise the critical issue of whether or not and to what degree such graced freedom is evident in the *ekklēsia* as an ontological reality. Do the actions of the church/Church give concrete testimony to the presence of graced freedom in the body and as the reality of the individual member, or are such actions reflective of a kind of liberty that is foreign to a fuller understanding of exactly what constitutes graced freedom in the *ekklēsia* as the body of Christ?

We will argue that there is, at present and in the contemporary church/Church, a greater sense of liberty than there is manifestation and expression of graced freedom. Such liberty is evident as an imprecise understanding of why the church/Church exists, how she is to approach decision making at every level, from whence she derives her purpose for existence, under whose authority she continues to exist as an event of free obedience, and what is, de facto, the exact nature of the message she is called, established, and commissioned to proclaim, and exactly why graced freedom is essential to the church/Church as *ekklēsia,* that is, as event, not merely as an institution or local organizational structure.

Are these mere generalizations that have no bearing on the day-to-day realities of the contemporary church/Church? We presume that there will be those who will think so; but we doubt that such contention will come from any pastor who, like the author of this essay, has devoted more

Introduction

than thirty years of life to the church/Church, and has witnessed a slow but evident diminishment of the centrality of this body as *ekklēsia*, together with significant and irregular changes in the body of believers over the last three decades. The concepts of a culture enamored with the ideology of self-directive free will, with individualization, relativism, pluralism, and with a growing indifference toward all claims to authority and indisputable truth claims, has not stopped short at entrance to the doors of the church/Church and her membership.

Even the leadership of the church/Church is not reluctant to employ and apply the mechanisms of culture, society, and business to the decision-making processes and planning of particular ministries in the life of the church/Church. And while such phenomena disclose a certain acculturation of the church/Church, the larger concern of this essay is to demonstrate those ways in which this also discloses a fascination with and conviction regarding the supreme value of liberty to the whole of church/Church in every aspect of her life, rather than an embrace of graced freedom as essential to the event of *ekklēsia*.

Furthermore, there is another manifestation of liberty evident in the church/Church—and in particular in the United States—that is equally disturbing, only because it has proven, as a misconception, to wreck havoc on the order (technically, the polity) of the local congregation and its essential associations with the one, holy, catholic, and apostolic *ekklēsia*. We refer to the way in which a democratic ideology has taken hold of the mind-set of many if not most of the members of the church/Church—and that, regardless of confessional position!

This phenomenon is most glaringly evident in Roman Catholic church/Church in North America, where each individual deems it appropriate to express his or her individuality, as liberty, in what should be (so they believe) a democratically administered organization (that is to say—the Church), as is any other similar voluntary organization in this nation. The voices of authority, the voice of Bishop, Magisterium, or Pope, whenever perceived to be in direct conflict with the rights of individual expression of liberty (and therefore undemocratic) are opposed with all the rigor one expects to witness in rebellion against a tyrannical oppressor; and it is troubling to hear members of Roman Catholic congregations refer to the authority of the Church in just such accusatory language. However, those who belong to any one of a number of Protestant churches can take no satisfaction in pointing an accusing finger at their Roman Catholic

Introduction

brothers and sisters, as this phenomenon is by no means restricted to the Roman Catholic churches; it can be discovered in almost any form of Christian church/Church and confessional body. While this may well be an expression of liberty as understood in a constitutional framework, it is far from that graced freedom which is the hallmark of the *ekklēsia*, genuine Christian discipleship, service to Christ through free obedience to Christ and his gospel, and serves as the heart and soul of an evangelical theology of freedom *for* humanity.

While we will address the following in greater detail in a later chapter, for now let us note how the apostle Paul writes, "Now the Lord is the Spirit, and where the Spirit of the Lord is, there is freedom" (2 Cor. 3:17). Not liberty, which is not to be found in the New Testament (with the possible exception of the derivatives, liberator/liberation), but freedom (Gk. *eleutheria*, et.al.)[4] and of a very particular kind![5] This essay is an attempt to

---

4. "The NT sees that retreat into inwardness does not in fact bring freedom. Existence is inwardly defective, so that to take oneself in hand is simply to grasp a defective existence. Faced with a lost existence, we can come to ourselves only by subjecting our own will to the will of another. We achieve self-control by letting ourselves be controlled. Concretely, *eleutheria* in the NT is freedom from sin (Rom. 6:18), the law (Rom. 7:3-4; Gal. 2:4), and death (Rom. 6:21-22; 8:21). It is freedom from an existence that in sin leads to the law of death. Existing in sin, we are its slaves (Rom. 6:20). The result is anarchy (Rom. 6:19). This means surrender to craving of the *sárx* that is triggered by the law (Rom. 6:12). The law is intended for good, expressing God's claim, but in our sinful existence it brings sin to light by mediating sinful affections. It is an occasion for self-seeking love of life that misuses the claim of God . . . Freedom, then, means freedom from the law as well as from sin, i.e., from the need to seek justification by the law. Freedom here is freedom from attempted autonomy, not by breaking the law, but by fulfilling our own interpretation of it in following our own needs, and doing our own will, by what seems to be an honest effort to do God's will. Freedom from the law means freedom from moralism, from self-lordship before God in the guise of serious and obedient responsibility" (*Theological Dictionary of the New Testament*, 225).

5. "How is this freedom achieved? The primary answer is: 'By the act of Christ.' Christ has made us free (Gal. 5:1). The reference here is to the event of the life that he offered up vicariously in obedience to God's will (cf. Gal. 3:13; 4:4). Our freedom is not an existential return to the soul. The Son makes us free (John 8:36). The secondary answer is: 'By the gospel call.' We are called to freedom (Gal. 5:13). This is a call to the act of Christ which is the basis of a new life in freedom. The life-giving Spirit of Jesus is present in the call (Rom. 8:2), advancing the claim of God's act in Christ, and making possible the true fulfillment of what the law demands as the will of God (Rom. 8:3ff.) . . . In the Spirit of Christ's own freedom, we find our own freedom . . . How do we bring this freedom to expression? The answer is: in love, i.e., not in isolation but in a life with others. We find freedom in service, in yielding our lives to the divinely demanded righteousness of love of God and neighbor (Rom. 6:18ff.). Freedom comes to expression in righteous acts of many different kinds (Gal. 5:22). Being free, we accept civil obedience (Mt. 17:24ff.;

xvii

Introduction

re-educate the church/Church in what is, perhaps, one of her most sterling characteristics in Christ—her graced freedom *for* obedience to God and in service to humanity as the unique characteristic of her being as *ekklēsia*. So that there can be no mistake or misunderstanding from the beginning, we evidently refer to that graced freedom revealed in all its fullness (i.e., *pleroma*) in Jesus Christ—ontologically and as redemptive event, and subsequently and by virtue of his gracious conferral of the Holy Spirit, in its fullness (*pleroma*) of the *ekklēsia* as well—ontologically and as event.

It could be rightly said that this proposal is Christological ecclesiology; and yet it would be equally appropriate to the argument of this essay to affirm that it is also and at the same time ecclesiological Christology. There will be no apology (in the theological sense of the word) made for this in the body of the essay as the essay itself is an attempt at such an apologetic; we believe that what the contemporary church/Church needs most at present is the reclamation and reaffirmation of the fact that she has no reality other than that which is conferred upon her by the living Lord Christ; Christological ecclesiology and ecclesiological Christology, in tandem, are considered essential to such reclamation and reaffirmation. This is not, however, to vacate the incipient ecclesiology in this essay of the presence and important—central!—role of the Holy Spirit in the being, sustenance, and event of the *ekklēsia* (recall the words of the apostle Paul quoted in the paragraph above); without the presence of the Spirit of Lord there would be no basis for a theology of freedom, and certainly not an evangelical theology of freedom for humanity.

We would also want to be clear that, while we have respect for the variety of what is often called Liberation Theology, we do not see any such theology as truly representative of an evangelical theology of freedom; primarily because of both the presuppositions underlying such theological expositions and exaggerated attention to the externals of the socio-political reality being addressed. In point of fact, we would assert that such theological explications advocate liberty as defined above and not evangelical freedom as an ontological reality. Such theological explanation is to be appreciated for the insights offered into the disposition of the poor and oppressed, the biblical mandate for justice, and the courage of expressed prophetic conviction. One can faithfully read the exodus narrative as a story of liberation from bondage, but such reading tends to undervalue

---

1 Pet. 2:13). We renounce rights for the sake of others (1 Cor. 9:19). We may forgo valid personal claims (1 Cor. 9:1)" (*Theological Dictionary of the New Testament*, 226).

the theological reality; the liberation of the Hebrew people from slavery in Egypt clearly reflected freedom from oppressive socio-political realities, yet the fundamental purpose for their being liberated was in order to establish freedom as the basis for obedience, worship, and service to the living God of Abraham, Isaac, and Jacob.

Nevertheless, we believe that the situation faced by the church/Church in North America is not one that can be addressed along socio-political lines, whether as the presupposition or as a viable proposed direction to resolution. With few exceptions, pastors in a multitude of settings in North America are seldom stunned by the plight of the poor and oppressed in any one of the congregations served or in the conditions of those living in the surrounding communities; most of the members of North American congregations are not struggling under a tyrannical regime, or severely limited by unjust laws, or wondering from where they will receive their next meal. And yet, even where such experience is the case of pastor and people (e.g., in urban centers or poor and economically depressed rural communities), the necessity for a theology of graced freedom is still a vital concern.

The last sentence of the previous paragraph simply highlights the importance of and need for the development of a theology of freedom in the North American context, among members of the church/Church, and as a proclamation of hope and promise to residents and non-believers of the wider community as well. While our culture and society experience liberty, whether one wishes to speak in terms of personal or national existence, what remains questionable is the degree to which individuals—and Christians in particular—are truly free in the ontological sense proposed in this essay. Based on experience both within and outside the church/Church, we would answer No, such freedom is foreign to members of the church/Church, and to people in general! For those who would respond, Of course I am free to do whatever I please, and to make choices for myself and at my own discretion, we would reply by advocating that such is not the deeper form of evangelical graced freedom extended to us in, with, and for Christ Jesus, but is in reality merely another manifestation of liberty in the socio-political realm.

True graced freedom, as advocated in this essay, must come from beyond us, it cannot be a reality we can secure or achieve for ourselves or through the machinations of human culture or society, simply because it is of a far higher, and at the same time deeper, reality than that which is readily at hand. The origin of such ontological freedom is transcendent

Introduction

and comes to us purely as a gift of grace from a loving God. Such freedom is not devoid of authority; rather such freedom perceives a transcendent authority to be an essential aspect of and necessary to the maintenance and sustainability of graced freedom.

Free obedience is given to such authority because the recipient acknowledges how, in faith and *a priori*, this genuine freedom has come to him or her as a gift of grace, maintained under the direct supervision of the Holy Spirit of the triune God. It is free as a manifestation of relational existence in, with, and for Christ, and obedience is a manifestation of love and gratitude for the graced freedom received. The presence of such graced freedom necessitates a continuing and maturing relationship with God in Christ; otherwise, this freedom will soon wither, leaving the formally freed person more susceptible to the bondage of sin as manifest in the numerous machinations of the principalities and powers. As actuality that must be constantly nurtured and nourished in the *ekklēsia*, this graced freedom is, in and of itself, an event in both outward and inward realities.

We learn of this ontological freedom from the evangelical witness of both Old and New Testaments, and acknowledge it to be supremely revealed in the person and work of Christ Jesus. And as we cannot speak of the person and work of Christ in isolation one from the other, neither can we speak of this graced freedom in terms other then ontological and manifest as event-full action(s). We refer to this gracious reality as graced freedom in order to differentiate it from all other expressions of freedom— for example, human freedom or political freedom. While such orders have their own intrinsic value, the ontological freedom of which we speak is born in an engagement with the Christ who incarnates and brings such freedom from the Father and in the power of the Holy Spirit, and confers the same on humanity; such engagement is made possible through the *ekklēsia* in both the reading and hearing of Holy Scripture, in proclamation as the Word of God, in the worship life of the *ekklēsia*, and in her fundamental configuration of the *missio Dei*.

Therefore, we cannot speak of such freedom in the absence of grace and faith in both the origin and continuance of such freedom in both the individual believer and the *ekklēsia*. From beginning to end (*telos*) this freedom is the act of God in Christ in the power of the Holy Spirit. The reality of this ontological freedom, as the redemption, renewal, and re-establishment of the true *anthropos* (in Christ, the New Adam), is also and at the widest

Introduction

dimension imaginable, what makes this an evangelical theology of freedom for humanity.

It is more than appropriate, even at this introductory level, to raise the question as to why this particular form of freedom should be vital for us today. What is it about our contemporary cultural, social, and spiritual matrix that necessitates an exploration of and proposal for this form of freedom? In brief, we contend that while our world is awash in select forms of liberty that have, perhaps, provided latitude for self-expression, self-enrichment, and self-assertion, we are not free in the deepest and most reflective sense of the term. In fact we would argue there is a growing sense in which more and more people are struggling to overcome a very real and very frightening form of bondage; despite all protestations to the contrary, people are not living lives that demonstrate the contentment, sense of fulfillment, and beauty of ontological freedom.

Tentatively we can list some forms of such bondage as New Age spiritualities, fashion, sports of all kinds, entertainment, reality TV, casinos, overindulgence, all pornographic materials, texting, cell phone addiction, abuse of drugs and overuse of alcohol; the list could be extended to include far more lethal manifestations of this same bondage. The essence of this bondage will be explored and discussed in a later chapter of this essay as having both internal and external dimensions; in the more traditional language of theology, such bondage could be considered under the rubric of sinful existential reality and temptation to sin. And yet, what is central to the diagnosis of the essence of the dilemma this proposal will address is the far larger issue of the loss of humanity, or better said, the loss of human dignity as *imago Dei*; a loss that is so prevalent in the world today its manifestations need not be detailed.

As a generality it can be said that pastors are concerned with the humanity of those they have been called and charged to serve in Christ; that is to say, even at the level of the individual member, pastors are serving, providing care, and offering counsel with the desire to enrich the integrity of the individual, as representative of *anthropos* (as *imago Dei* and as a new creation in Christ), which is so often brought into question and/or injured in a culture and society that can be and often is de-humanizing in so many ways and at so many levels. Beyond the individual, the pastor is concerned to preach and teach the evangelical word that will provide his or her people with the proper biblical-theological perspective on the essential nature of human dignity and how they are—as *ekklēsia*—called to actively preserve

Introduction

such dignity, or to call for the reclamation of human dignity, wherever it has been brought into question or perhaps even threatened with extinction. This, then, is a disclosure of graced freedom as freedom for humanity!

However, it is incumbent upon one who holds the pastoral office to preach and teach the evangelical word for purposes that exceed mere attainment of knowledge of Holy Scripture and *parádosis* (i.e., tradition); in reliance upon the event of the Holy Spirit, the pastor preaches and teaches for transformation and, as we want to contend, the renewal and reaffirmation of freedom for humanity in the presence of God. This transformation is also an event in that it can only be attributed to the active presence and engagement of the Holy Spirit and is processive; this is the axis point at which we encounter the dialectic spoken of in a previous paragraph. The renewal and reaffirmation of humanity (as *imago Dei*) must be a process, not only by virtue of the active engagement (i.e., event) of the Holy Spirit, but also because this individual (and *ekklēsia*) is subject to the paradox of existence in faith (that which the Protestant reformers referred to as *simul justus et peccator*).

Should this proposal hold, it will place the *ekklēsia* in one of the most significant roles it could possibly have in relation to the socio-political and cultural orders; it could herald the reestablishment of the essential nature of the *ekklēsia* as she relates to both (and more) of these orders. Actually, it should be historically evident that this has been the role to which the *ekklēsia* has been called to serve her Savior and Lord, and therefore the world, from the exact moment of her birth in the event of Pentecost and under the dominion of the Holy Spirit as her Lord. From the beginning, the *ekklēsia* has been called to proclaim a glorious freedom for humanity revealed and given to and for the world in the incarnation, life, ministry, passion, death, resurrection, and ascension of Jesus Christ, which is the substance of the evangelical word. This freedom for humanity established the *ekklēsia* as essential to the proclamation and promotion of justice (as defined by Christ and his gospel); it was and remains this mandate that also and often places the *ekklēsia* in a paradoxical position vis-à-vis those orders we have already mentioned, and others as well. An acculturated church/Church has, unfortunately, been compromised by virtue of her dependence upon something—some ideological or sociological mandate—other than the proclamation and promotion of that form of graced freedom which has been her birthright (by grace) and is demanded of her as free obedience in the powerful presence of the Holy Spirit.

Introduction

Graced freedom is freedom from captivity to sin so that it might be freedom for worship of and obedience to the One True God in tri-unity; not merely worship as ritual engagement and enactment on Sunday morning, but equally, and as the word itself implies, the work of the people of God in the world, for the world, and to the glory of God. Whether one refers to the mandates of any single denominational body or to those of organizations such as the WCC Life and Work commission of the ecumenical movement, such mandates often focus attention on areas of the socio-political order that demonstrate de-humanizing characteristics and need to be addressed in and through the *ekklēsia* to the world as unacceptable in light of Christ and his gospel mandate. Such mandates have integrity and merit to the degree that they promote graced freedom, and not some form of socio-cultural or political liberation that simply cannot compare to the profound proclamation of an ontological freedom that need not exclude the socio-political order.

The freedom for humanity incarnate in Christ Jesus and given witness to in his gospel must always be seen as the form of graced freedom that transcends all humanly fabricated forms of freedom—regardless of their merit! The pastor in his or her study, pulpit, and lectern is called to proclaim this form of graced freedom with all the wisdom, insight, and integrity at his or her command (and let us never forget, under the presence and power of the Holy Spirit). Whether in the seminary classroom or holding pastoral office in the local *ekklēsia*, this is the audience we would hope to address and engage in open and constructive conversation.

We suppose someone could raise the question as to what makes this a theological expression distinctive to the context of North America, as it would seem from all that has been stated thus far, this same proposal could have been drafted on almost any continent and in almost any country in the world. And we would respond that what makes this proposal unique is that it derives from the context of the local church/Church in the United States, and not merely as a theological exploration of some cultural issue endemic to North America; it is a proposal for a critically constructive way in which theology can be done—from a pastoral perspective—and in relation to the current crises facing the church/Church in the United States. We have attempted, in this introduction, to address (even if only in a tentative fashion) one aspect of the crises, by making reference to the numerous ways in which a particular and limited understanding of liberty has adversely

Introduction

affected the identity, worship life, concept of discipleship, overall discernment, and theological self-understanding of the local church/Church.

If we could make an educated guess as to why Dr. Barth expressed the hope for an evangelical theology of freedom for humanity to arise from the native theological soils of the United States, we would suggest that, as was so often true of his insights, subsequent to his visit to the US, Barth saw with clarity that one of the more important issues facing the church/Church in the US is a tendency to confuse socio-political and cultural realities with the gospel as the purpose for the existence of the church/Church in North America. This has become abundantly clear in the current race for the presidency of the United States (2012), and the misappropriation and misuse of Christian language and technical theological terminology by politicians who have had little or no training in the complexities of theological explication, and yet are considered to express positions that are legitimate to both the theology of the Christian faith and, at the same time, demonstrate a knowledge of theological realities.

It is also possible that Karl Barth perceived, what is often and mistakenly referenced as the Constitutional separation of church and state, as fundamentally problematic to the degree that such separation could imply a disallowance or rejection of the legitimacy of a theological voice in the public square; therefore a theology of freedom taking its substance and direction from the evangelical testimony of evangelists, prophets, and apostles, could then enable the *ekklēsia* to speak with a more distinctive voice, a more concisely framed theological message, to those residents of the public square. Of course, we can only surmise that these (and no doubt other) reasons were behind the expressed hope of Dr. Barth; perhaps our Lord will grant the grace to ask Dr. Barth when we meet with him at Table in the coming kingdom of God!

Finally, without any equivocation we reassert that this essay is Christologically centered, and is so primarily because the resurrected and reigning Lord Christ stands at the horizon of human history casting a long and evident shadow of grace over all reality, the reality of human freedom being no exception. We cannot, at least from within the context of a pastoral theology, speak meaningfully of an evangelical freedom that is not grounded in Christological verities; Jesus Christ himself being the embodiment of the "Good News," the gospel, in essence, offering testimony to the Truth, and in Truth there is graced freedom (see John 8:32). It is in Jesus Christ we witness the fullness of that graced freedom revealed in human flesh and from the human side as freedom for obedience, worship, and service to the one true God; it is in Jesus Christ we witness graced freedom as the consummation of love (as *agapē*) for God and neighbor, which is essential to enrichment of communal harmony and therefore revelatory of the coming kingdom of God; it is through Jesus Christ that freedom is proclaimed and conferred in the form of God's Truth (i.e., the *evangel*); and it is in Jesus Christ that his body—the *ekklēsia*—proclaims that same *evangel* which, through the empowerment of the Holy Spirit is Word of God, continuing to spread the promise of graced freedom, as reality, in the lives of those who hear, acknowledge, and confess the Truth of God.

THE CHAPTERS AHEAD

In this section of the introduction we provide an outline of the chapters to follow, by merely touching on the subject of each chapter. In this way we hope to provide a vehicle through which the reader can select to read particular chapters. The proposal does necessitate and involve a continuity of argument, which is best appreciated by reading each chapter in order; nevertheless, the chapters have also been written in such a fashion that they can stand on their own merit, should you desire to read at random. It should be stated at this juncture that throughout all that follows we make use of the phrase *evangelical freedom* when referencing the wider context of biblical-theological witness to graced freedom, and the phrase *graced freedom* when referencing that form of freedom which is established, sustained, and ultimately fulfilled by God and God alone, in and through the power of the Holy Spirit.

We make use of the word *essay* for this text only because we envision a book as having greater depth and a more thorough investigation of all of the related issues relevant to the subject at hand. An essay (at least to our understanding) is offered as a prelude to what could become a book, should there be significant dialogue to warrant such an expansion of the topic; for now, we are quite content to provide an essay!

Remaining consistent to our proposal of an evangelical freedom we must avoid the temptation to limit ourselves to a select number of biblical passages that speak directly to the issue at hand, as if proof-texting were an honored method for theological explication as an evangelical modus operandi! There are paradigmatic passages that we will consider applicable to the proposal; but on the whole we will consider the continuous thread of revelation running throughout the Old and New Testament witness to God and the plan of redemption as far more reliable in supporting the proposal. The affirmation of evangelical freedom cannot be restricted to the witness of the New Testament alone, for the simple reason that it is also evidenced (if only as proleptic reality) in the Old Testament witness, and in particular in the word of the prophets.

Chapter one will explore the biblical basis for a diagnosis of the fundamental problem for *anthropos*, which is not external to human being (ontological reality), but is an internal reality and as a direct result of a tragedy that has corrupted—no, has completely disfigured!—*anthropos* as God created him/her/them to be (i.e., the *imago Dei*). The fact that this horrific tragedy could neither be remedied nor repaired by virtue of any single human endeavor will be annunciated as well, together with the first hints of the proposed graced freedom as promise (and proleptic reality), which are evidenced in select narratives of the Old Testament that are paradigmatic in character.

Chapter two will explore those ways in which Israel, as a covenant partner, demonstrated the dialectic of obedience-disobedience to God and to the Torah (as the external manifestation of what is required of those who are genuinely free) and restoration (i.e., the redemptive actions of God) as renewal and reaffirmation of graced freedom by way of repentance, covenant renewal, and a return to obedience to God through confirmation of and conformation to the Torah. This will be considered under the rubric of a proleptic recapitulation of graced freedom for humanity, which is the purpose behind the call of God to and establishment of Israel as a people—an *ekklēsia*. In this chapter we will take a close and careful look at some of the prophetic literature as the word disclosing the intention of God for the *ekklēsia* as a communion whose purpose is fulfilled only and insofar as she declares the gospel of God and demonstrates the graced freedom bestowed by God as a freedom for humanity.

Chapter three will open an exploration of the New Testament, beginning with a discussion of the central importance of the characters of John the Baptist and Mary the mother of Christ as primary witnesses to that form of graced freedom which is the essential mark of *anthropos* as God created it to be, and as lives demonstrating the essential characteristics of graced freedom in their life-transformed testimony to what is to be revealed in Christ. Both John and Mary offer clear evidence of, again, a proleptic manifestation of that form of graced freedom to which one bears definitive and prophetic witness, and the other unequivocal ontological witness. As an added benefit, we are hopeful that the discussion of Mary, as *theotokos*, will once again provide her with the place she is, regrettably, too often denied in much of Protestant theology.

In Chapter four we turn our attention to the writings of the Apostle Paul and to selections from the Pastoral Epistles as well. It will be argued that the writings of the Apostle, and select Pastorals, are informed and shaped throughout by a clear and concise evangelical theology of freedom for humanity. This evangelical theology for humanity is not to be thought of as a replacement for the essential focus of faith in God; rather, because this is graced freedom, it can recognize, acknowledge, honor, and promote no other basis for such freedom save that which God and God alone has made possible. The evangelical theology of graced freedom annunciated by Paul and others is the dramatic proclamation of that Word which, under the power of the Holy Spirit, becomes event and as event makes possible the beginning of such ontological freedom for those who both hear and receive him who is this graced freedom incarnate, and give their lives to obedience, worship, and service.

In Chapter five we turn attention to the Book of Revelation as the paradigmatic text par excellance for the development of a theology of freedom for humanity. All strange imagery and apocalyptic conceptualizations aside, this narrative is a wonderfully prophetic affirmation of that graced freedom Christ came to assert as the basis for genuine *anthropos*. The fact that John has placed this futuristic scenario in direct relation to current issues facing a persecuted and de-humanized population and *ekklēsia* in his own time, is fruitful for the development of a theology of freedom that looks to the future, as well as the past and present. The Book of Revelation cannot be properly appreciated as theological proclamation of genuine freedom, as a gift of grace, so long as it remains encumbered with the silly and presumptuous forms of interpretation made popular in contemporary media; what we hope to provide is a far more faithful and profoundly hopeful engagement with this same biblical material.

Chapter six will cover, what we consider to be, novel terrain; in this chapter we will contemplate those ways in which an evangelical theology of freedom for humanity, in order to speak to the catholic *ekklēsia*, must be ecumenical in character—or at the very least, speak to what could reasonably be considered ecumenical concerns. We will also suggest those ways in which an evangelical theology of freedom for humanity could play a role in advancing the present impasse in the ecumenical endeavor, by revisiting the role of the *ekklēsia* as the free community of freed persons, seeking greater freedom for the whole of humanity.

In the Conclusion we will summarize the argument made throughout this essay and provide indications—hints, if you will—to those ways in which this particular proposal for an evangelical theology of freedom could shape and inform the services to Christ as offered by the one who is in preparation to hold, or currently holds, the pastoral office.

1

The Foundation and Fundamental Problem

"In the beginning..."

ANY DISCUSSION OF GENUINE evangelical freedom must begin at the beginning, at least in the biblical and theological sense of the term *beginning* (i.e., genesis). The reasoning behind this approach should be evident to anyone who holds strong conviction regarding the origin of the evangel (the good news) as having a direct and irrefutable relationship to select passages and narratives, and to the richly variegated theological reflections of the Old Testament. If, as is our position, graced freedom can only be rightly understood and appreciated as having its origin in the will of a loving, merciful, and righteous Lord God, as a revelation of the immanent Trinity, and in the purposes for which God created *anthropos* (as biblically represented by Adam and Eve) and the whole of the created order, then our attention must first be given to select texts in which we first receive word of this glorious and gracious event.

Our attention will be given to those portions of the Book of Genesis bearing directly on our proposal of a biblical witness to graced freedom. But we must first make clear that our task is not to write a commentary (in the traditional sense) on the Book of Genesis, as a commentary would take us into the intricacies of word study, textual variations, and so on, and would therefore distract us from the more immediate concern of our study.

That is not to say that such commentary has been ignored in the process of preparing this and the following chapters, dealing as they do with particular paradigms or passages of Holy Scripture, necessitating conscientious attention (on the part of the author of this essay) to the field of exegesis and biblical commentary. We are tracing what we envision to be the contours of graced freedom at the heart of the evangelical witness to the saga of salvation history as recorded throughout the Old and New Testaments, from creation to consummation and in the central revelation of God in Christ. Our approach demands a certain attention to key pericopes, paradigmatic narratives, and passages that can be said to bear specific theological witness, thematically, to the creation, continuance, and consummation of graced freedom, which also requires us to approach Scripture more broadly than would be appropriate or responsible if these chapters were intended to constitute an exegetical commentary on Holy Scripture. We have avoided the use of footnoted references, which would be warranted in a more technical form; our concern is for a more creative, theological explication of each pericope or passage under discussion as each speaks directly (or indirectly) to the purpose at hand. The use of *creative* in the last sentence should not be misconceived as a theological explication cut adrift from appreciation for the rigors of exegetical engagement; however, since we hope to address a readership beyond that of the more academic audience, we determined it best to limit—if not to avoid altogether—the more academic apparatus associated with biblical commentary.

CREATION AND GRACED FREEDOM

"In the beginning, God created the heavens and earth. The earth was formless and void, and darkness was over the surface of the deep, and the Spirit of God was moving over the surface of the waters. Then God said, 'Let there be . . .'" (Gen. 1:3a). With these words we are introduced to the first act of God in creation of the heavens and the earth, which is also and at the same time the first disclosure of graced freedom conferred as an act of God; God had no need to create that which would be external (though eternally related) to God-self. This singular act of grace is a manifestation of the ground for the covenantal nature of the relationship between God and creation (we are not yet speaking of Adam/Eve); it is also a manifestation of the gift of freedom in the establishment of creation as separate from and yet eternally related to the triune God. Only a creation imbued with freedom, as an event of grace, could be actualized in the splendor God intended; a creation without such imbued freedom would remain confined in a manner associated with sin and its consequences (i.e., sin as the distortion, or better said, the contradiction, and thereby the abolition, of graced freedom). To speak of the earth as formless and empty is to imply the absence of freedom prior to the Word of God bringing all things into an ordered existence; the Word of God brings freedom as event and, whenever issued, is always fruitful in giving graced freedom new birth. Chaos itself is prior to and implies the absence of graced freedom; in bringing order in the singular event of creation, God demonstrates that aspect of his will that intends harmony, wholeness, and the integrity of the creation as disclosive of graced freedom as essential to the welfare and further enrichment of the created order.

When the author of Genesis testifies to the consecutive affirmation of God (i.e., And God saw that it was good), the reference to *good* implies that the intention of God, for any one aspect of the created order, was clearly manifest in the function of that specific order; there was no gap (if you will) between the purpose for which any one aspect of creation was spoken into existence and its function in fulfilling the purpose for which God intended its existence. There was an evident manifestation of the freedom with which God had graced the created order in the fact that each feature was said to be good. The Word of God is also that creative Word which alone confers graced freedom. The conferral of freedom was, therefore, endemic by virtue of the creative and spoken Word of God; the Word of God (understood here as the second person of the Trinity) granted as grace that freedom by which the creation would remain obedient and faithful to its divinely intended purpose; one of the more severe consequences of Adam's fall would be the forfeiture of this graced freedom, together with the concomitant distortion of the created order at the material level of existence and the incapacity for obedience at the level of human response to God's will.

> Then God said, "Let Us make man in Our image, according to Our likeness; and let them rule over the fish of the sea and over the birds of the sky and over the cattle and over all the earth, and over every creping thing that creeps on the earth." God created man in His own image; in the image of God He created him; male and female He created them.
>
> God blessed them; and God said to them, "Be fruitful and multiply, and fill the earth, and subdue it; and rule over the fish of the sea and over the birds of the sky and over every living thing that moves on the earth." (Gen. 1:26–28)

A Pastoral Proposal for an Evangelical Theology of Freedom

The creation of *anthropos* as male and female affirms the *imago Dei* as a relational category; male and female share a common bond of communal identification in that all nature of personal fulfillment is dependent upon the employment, acknowledgement, and faithful engagement of graced freedom in the establishment and continual nurturing of what it means to be "human" created *imago Dei*. Without this graced freedom the "male" and "female" would have been incapable of engaging in that form of relational existence that alone provides the environment for the fulfillment of self in, with, and through the welfare of the other; it would not be possible to "love"—as the basis of both covenantal and communal existence—if such "love" did not arise from that graced freedom conferred by God as an ontological reality. The desire to find completion in nurturing the fulfillment of the other would only be possible as the externalization of that graced freedom, which also and at the same time enables communal welfare; the "male" and "female" are not so much corresponding persons, as they are communal partners in the complementary enactment of graced freedom. In the enactment of graced freedom "male" and "female" discover the enrichment of life as affirmed by their Creator (i.e., be fruitful and multiply); it is only with such graced freedom that "male" and "female" can subdue and rule within the whole of created order without imposition of selfish or self-serving will-to-power. The graced freedom they have been given is the sole basis upon which they can oversee the welfare of the created order—as good stewards—caring for a multiplicity of creatures, animate subjects and inanimate objects, with a love, freedom, and devotion that can be said to impersonate that of their Creator.

What is being affirmed here is that *anthropos*—created "male" and "female"—was not given to subdue and rule the created order in such a fashion as to contradict the presence of graced freedom, as if they were given a divine mandate to rule the created order with a heavy hand and solely to the benefit of their own appetites! The office of obedience they received was a fundamental responsibility for maintenance of the welfare of the semblance of graced freedom within the created order, a genuine respect for the manner in which the Creator's intent was to enlarge the shared beauty of the relational bond between all living things that would assure the enlargement and enrichment of graced freedom throughout the created order.

Regardless of the authorial intent of the divine command to *anthropos* that they—and all other creatures—restrict themselves to that form of food that was from seed-bearing plants and from every tree whose fruit contains seed, this divine command implies that the taking of any form of animate life would be the misuse of graced freedom. One cannot comprehend this word from the Lord as anything less than a direct command, and therefore calling for an expression of graced freedom in obedience to God's command. To take the life of another animate being, for purposes of self-sustenance, would be a violation of the command, and therefore demonstrate the relinquishment of graced freedom in the desire to impose one's own will on another being, since one cannot (in the context of the narrative as it stands) speak meaningfully of any sentient creature willingly offering its life for the well-being of another. As we will soon see, one of the first casualties of Adam's fall from graced freedom is the Lord's sacrifice of one of his beloved creatures to "cover" the shame of Adam and Eve; in this singular act of divine compassion, one can overhear the sorrowful voice of graced freedom's demise! It can be stated that as broadly as graced freedom animated the whole of creation and every creature, so extensively did the effect of Adam's fall from graced freedom adversely affect that same graced freedom, and at every level of existence.

Yet before taking up discussion of Adam's fall from graced freedom, we must turn briefly to exposition of the second narrative of creation as found in the Book of Genesis (2:15–25):

> The Lord God took the man and put him in the garden of Eden to cultivate it and keep it. The Lord God commanded the man, saying, "From any tree of the garden you may eat freely; but from the tree of the knowledge of good and evil you shall not eat, for in the day that you eat from it you will surely die." Then the Lord God said, "It is not good for the man to be alone; I will make him a helper suitable for him." . . . So the Lord God caused a deep sleep to fall upon the man, and he slept; then He took one of his ribs and closed up the flesh at that place. Then the Lord God fashioned into a woman the rib which He has taken from the man, and brought her to the man. The man said: This is now bone of my bone and flesh of my flesh; She shall be called Woman, Because she was taken from Man. For this reason a man shall leave his father and mother, and be joined to his wife; and they become one flesh. And the man and his wife were both naked and were not ashamed.

Central to this version of the creation of Adam is the importance given to the necessity for companionship as an essential characteristic of what it means to be a creature given existence for the sole purpose of engaging in the covenantal relationship established by the Lord God as the foundation for the relational expression of graced freedom. God creates Adam

A Pastoral Proposal for an Evangelical Theology of Freedom

in covenantal existence and for the purposes of faithfulness as a covenant creature; this covenantal characteristic defines Adam at both the individual (and as soon becomes apparent) and communal levels of existence. As has been affirmed by biblical scholars, the naming of the creatures is, perhaps, a demonstration of Adam's lordship over creation as the divinely established steward of the created order; but it is also a prelude to the recognition of the painful void that remains in the life of Adam, evident in the limitations imposed on his communion with all other creatures, by virtue of the existing ontological contrast between Adam and them, a contrast that cannot be altered.

The phrase "it is not good for man to be alone" sounds at first blush like an observation made on some unspoken aspect of Adam's behavior, when in fact it is more likely a theological affirmation of the need for Adam to be defined by the boundary of another's existence—one who would serve as both complement and contrast to Adam, and in that same necessary duality establish the basis for communal harmony. Here the use of *not good* seems to suggest something of incompleteness to the being of Adam; not an imperfection in his being, so much as incapacity to be all God intends for Adam as a covenant partner.

The creation of the woman from the rib of Adam would imply an immediate and essential bond between them, even before Adam had awakened to acknowledge the same, evident in the exuberant words, on his first view of Eve, representing an impassioned exclamation: "This one, at last, is bone of my bone and flesh of my flesh." Each of the two, Adam and Eve, have as their first object of faithfulness, covenantal obedience to the Lord God; and out of that covenantal existence arises the commitment to a similar obligation in the relationship they will then share. The expression of graced freedom, as obedience to the first covenantal relationship (i.e., with the Lord God), will be manifest in their capacity to enrich and enlarge both the complementary and contrasting characteristics of their divinely created covenant partner (i.e., they become one flesh).

When considered within the framework of human communal existence, harmony, in its essentials, is evident not so much as the absence of conflict as it is in the capacity to express graced freedom in obedience to God and in seeking the welfare and enlargement of life for the other; this is but a reflection—but a genuine reflection!—of that far more transcendent freedom with which the Lord God engages in the lives of both creature and creation. The covenant has established the parameters of conferred freedom for obedience as well as for the establishment and enrichment of communal existence; graced freedom finds its primary expression within the established boundaries of the covenantal relationship with the living God (what could be called the vertical dimensional dynamic) and only secondarily within communal realities (what could be called the horizontal dimensional dynamic). In this passage marriage becomes one of the more evident covenantal contexts in which graced freedom is expressed within the relationship between male and female, as one that promises enrichment and limited fulfillment of life.

The reference to the two becoming one flesh should not be understood solely in terms of sexual intimacy, nor as affirming a form of existence in which the uniqueness and contrasting characteristics of the individual are sacrificed to the bonding of communal realities; in either case, such an understanding would bring graced freedom into serious question and, perhaps, even present a confused if not distorted image of the gracious intent of God in creating *anthropos* as male and female. Just as *anthropos* has been created a covenantal-communal creature, whose very existence necessitates the expression of graced freedom in relation to the Other or other, so this affirmation of one flesh implies a commonality of focus and intent in covenantal regard for the welfare and enrichment of the other partner in every aspect that is essential to his or her well-being, and to nurture in him or her that form of free expression of "self" that brings honor to the Creator. Should the reference be to the marital covenant (as is likely the case), the implications extend far beyond the boundaries of any one marriage, pointing instead to "marriage" as that form of covenantal engagement intended by the Lord to exemplify the best employment of the graced freedom bestowed, as the context in which obedience—as respectful acknowledgment of shared accountability for the enrichment of the other before God—mirrors for the whole of creation the beauty of such graced freedom.

At this juncture it is necessary to recall the words of the apostle Paul to the Ephesians: "He who loves his wife loves himself. For no one ever hates his own flesh, but provides and cares for it, just as Christ does for the church, since we are members of His body" (Eph. 5:28b–29). While Paul is engaged in a discussion of analogy (marriage and the church), he apparently stresses the necessary connection between "love" and "covenantal obedience" to the intent of God for marriage (as well as the *ekklēsia*). At its best—in its fullness of expressed graced freedom—marriage is emblematic of that covenantal relationship with which Christ engages the *ekklēsia*, a relationship in which Christ seeks to nurture and enrich those expressions of graced freedom as rooted in a "love" that both transcends and is—by virtue of the Holy Spirit—embodied in the *ekklēsia,* even as it can be seen in the marital covenant as faithful to God's intent. Being a "member" of the "body of Christ" includes accountability for the spiritual enrichment and enlargement of the other(s), as an expression of *agapē* and graced freedom in obedience to the evident will of God for this "body" as the "body" of his Son! To treat a member of the *ekklēsia* with distain, disregard for his or her welfare, or—yes—with hatred, is not only an affront to the Lord, but manifests little more than the abolition of graced freedom and bondage to that which is contrary to God's will in every aspect of what it means to be a covenantal being (i.e., sin).

This "aside" brings us into the domain of that portion of the biblical narrative that provides evidence of how graced freedom was surrendered in the most subtle and yet the most disastrous of dialogical debates between Eve and that other creature, the serpent, (with Adam, no doubt, lurking somewhere within ear-shot); we delay in pronouncing the name of this other, as it bears all of the characteristics of calamity; simply recall the confrontation between Jesus and the Gerasene demoniac (see Luke 8.26–39) in which, when asked the tormentor's name, the being replied, Legion! Naming this malevolence is difficult because it seeks to remain anonymous and hidden in the shadows of the world and human living; it has no existence of its own and is merely a leach! We turn our attention now to that portion of the narrative which speaks of Adam and Eve as "fallen" from the gracious gift of an incomparable freedom!

THE ABOLITION OF GRACED FREEDOM

> Now the serpent was more crafty than any beast of the field which the Lord God had made. And he said to the woman, "Indeed, has God said, 'You shall not eat from any tree in the garden?'" The woman said to the serpent, "From the fruit of the trees of the garden we may eat; but from the fruit of the tree which is in the middle of the garden, God has said, 'You shall not eat it or touch it, or you will die.'" The serpent said to the woman, "You surely will not die! For God knows that in the day you eat from it your eyes will be opened, and you will be like God, knowing good and evil." When the woman saw that the tree was good for food, and that it was a delight to the eyes, and that the tree was desirable to

The Foundation and Fundamental Problem

make one wise, she took from its fruit and ate; and she also to her husband with her, and he ate. Then the eyes of both of them were opened, and they knew that they were naked; and they sewed fig leaves together and made themselves loin coverings.

Few passages of Scripture have received as much attention to etiological intent as the text that is before us; whether one's attention is directed to the origin of the "serpent" as symbolic of the cunning and wile of evil—the creatures mysterious capacity to strike the victim unawares, or at the most extreme, as the basis for pressing a form of misogynistic foolishness! However, when considered from the vantage point of graced freedom, this narrative unfolds a drama that stands in the foreground of salvation history, disclosing as it does both the essential nature of "sin" and the abolition of graced freedom, as the basis of covenantal obedience. It is in the subtlety of this story that one discovers the depth of the tragedy that is the defeat of graced freedom and the absurdity of both "evil" and "sin" as shadowed realities. We propose to explore and explicate this narrative as an etiology for the abolition of graced freedom, and, in all of the intricacy and suspense the story entails, elucidate those ways in which the story is a mirror image of the plight of the "fallen" human across the great span of generations. The ease with which Eve (and Adam) relinquish God's graced freedom is not only genuinely unsettling, but is also in its implications a warning to all those who assume that one can only surrender such graced freedom after a prolonged and dreadful battle with temptation.

The surrender of graced freedom begins, not with some dramatic demonstration of the power of temptation over the fragile nature of the vulnerable human soul, but with—what amounts to—a casual conversation, a kind of theological engagement, a discussion regarding the exact content and meaning of God's word, promise, and providential grace. For our purposes, there seems to be little value in entertaining an exploration of this passage as the "origin of evil," as this would merely distract us from following the narrative as it stands in its present canonical form. Nevertheless, we note that the serpent is referred to as a creature that God has made, which would imply that it was—like the rest of the created order—in its originality good (i.e., conforming to the purpose for which it was created) in the sight of God. It is critical to our purposes to see the manner in which the "serpent" was—as a good creature of the Lord—the first to surrender that freedom with which it was imbued at creation, in both its own participation in that which was contrary to its creaturely-covenantal

A Pastoral Proposal for an Evangelical Theology of Freedom

obedience to the will of God for its being, and in advancing that which would foreshadow the abolition of graced freedom on the part of Eve and Adam. What is dramatically demonstrated is the horrific manner in which freedom is the first casualty in the introduction of both temptation and consequent sin into the created order itself; the abolition of graced freedom on the part of Eve and Adam is a mirror image of this initial surrender of a sacred trust.

Considering, in more specific terms, the conversation that leads to this tragic event we begin, of course, with the serpent's counsel: "Indeed, has God said, 'You shall not eat from any tree of the garden?'" The absurdity of the query is patently evident; should Eve and Adam be prohibited from eating from any of the trees of the garden, they would perish! As of equal, if not surpassing importance, the question posed by the serpent directly contradicts the command of God (see Gen. 1:29–30); it is, in its essentials, the opposite of what God has graciously provided and commanded of his covenant partner. One should not be too hasty in criticizing Eve for failing to see the absurdity in the serpent's logic, as, with all genuine intent, she might have undertaken this conversation in order to defend the honor and integrity of God's word and providential intention; one could raise the question as to what constitutes the purpose of obedience (as graced freedom before God), if not a willingness to engage in apologetics!

Yet one readily sees the fallacy of such logic when considering the full reply offered by Eve to the serpent's query: "From the fruit of the trees of the garden we may eat; but from the fruit of the tree which is in the middle of the garden, God has said, 'You shall not eat from it or touch it, or you will die.'" If the serpent's question is an absurdity, the reply of Eve is equally telling. She has—for reasons that are not stated in the narrative—added to the command of the Lord; nowhere in the text thus far has there been any reference to "touching" the fruit of the tree in the midst of the garden as being equally forbidden. This additional wording heightens the demand of God's prohibition, making God's command almost as absurd in its implications as is the question of the serpent! Eve's editorializing of God's word also implies advancing beyond the boundary of her authority established by the Lord; in the misuse of her graced freedom she extends God's direct command with impunity (one recalls the stern admonition found at the close of John's Revelation, 22:18–19).

Now comes the moment of the turn, as the serpent uses words that directly countermand the word of God; he says to Eve, "You surely will not die." Graced freedom continues to hang in the balance, as the fact of Eve's continuing discussion—and even her unfortunate addition of wording to God's command—has not yet led to the surrender of such freedom. First the serpent, as a creature of God, further demonstrates its own capitulation of freedom as it engages in the "lie," which will remain at the heart of all manifestations of evil and for all time; the "lie" is fundamentally that God is himself untrustworthy, deceitful with his creatures, and intent on their obeying his will by use of threat—and not as the direct consequence of graced freedom. The "lie" is that one is truly "free" only to the extent that he or she has the "choice" to obey or follow his or her own path—or that suggested by another!

But the most insidious character of the "lie" as "lie" is found in the last words spoken by the serpent: "For God knows that in the day you eat from it your eyes will be opened, and you will be like God, knowing good and evil." Implicitly what we are given, via the rationale of the serpent, is the suggestion that God's will and command, as well as God's demand of obedience, are fundamentally based on God's insecurity in having his creatures share in knowledge that must be reserved for God alone, and not that the command regarding the tree in the midst of the garden was instituted by God for the welfare of Adam and Eve, whose obedience in graced freedom could have brought additional and even more abundant blessings to their shared life and that of every creature in their care. However, one is left with the open question: What was it, then, that literally pushed Eve over the point of no return, wherein she surrendered (and Adam with her) graced freedom for bondage (concurrent with sin)?

We would suggest that the answer is to be found in the comment of the serpent that Eve and Adam would be like God, knowing good and evil. In other words, where Adam and Eve had already been graced with having been created *imago Dei* (which, it must be stated, also and at the same time dismisses the likeness [Genesis 1.26!]—as an ontological reality—as somehow insufficient); what they reach for now is the attainment of a certain *kind* of knowledge—the disposition to determine what is the nature of both the good and the evil—a capability and authority attributable to God alone. The advantage of having such "knowledge" is not stated explicitly in the narrative; by implication it points to the uncontrolled desire to achieve the competence to judge between good and evil, as a transcendent characteristic, placing Eve and Adam "above" all other forms of created existence, and in the end deny the necessity *for* God and eliminate any relationship of obedience *to* God.

Here we witness the dramatic overreach of human pride and—at such great cost—posing as the implied action of "freedom of choice" (*de jure*) which is submission to the slavery of sin (*de facto*). Since the temptation comes from him who will soon receive the title the father of lies, it only stands to reason that surrender to this voice of disobedience (which is the ultimate "lie!") can only be understood as the surrender of graced freedom; there is genuine freedom only in Truth, and surrender to the "lie" is at once the loss, surrender, and tragic event of the abolition of graced freedom; this explication follows the argument of the apostle Paul as annunciated in his epistle to the Romans (1:24–25): "Therefore God gave them over in the lusts of their hearts . . . they exchanged the truth of God for a lie . . . !"

This dramatic turn of events, which ends with the acknowledgment of a sense of shame now evident in the covenantal relationship between Eve and Adam, and with testimony to their own sudden awareness of vulnerability as jeopardizing their covenanted connectedness (i.e., suddenly they see the other, not as complementary-contrast, but as a potential threat to exploiting both the individuality and self-expression of the other), ends with the singular response of the Lord God to each of the participants in this debacle—the serpent, Eve, and Adam—allotting to each a judgment that reflects their individual accountability for what has transpired, each bearing, not so much in the essential nature of their being, but rather as an external burden disclosing the loss of graced freedom (see Gen. 3:8–24). Buried within this same stretch of narrative (yet not so deep it cannot be heard) is a word of grace and promise—which has come to be called the *proto-euangelion*—the first hint of gospel: The Lord God said to the serpent, "I will put enmity between you and woman, between your seed and her seed. He shall bruise you on the head, and you shall bruise him on the heel" (Gen. 3.15). "Enmity" has now been introduced into an environment intended to birth and sustain harmony and wholeness in covenantal faithfulness; yes, between God and his covenant creatures (Adam and Eve, *anthropos* as male and female), but also between Adam and Eve and every living creature of the "Garden." From this point forward—until the coming of the Christ—graced freedom will be evident in fits and starts, with long lapses of disobedience and therefore—bondage. But the word of promise has been issued and God will always prove true to his word of grace; we will address this glorious redemption, restoration, and recapitulation in due time.

The Foundation and Fundamental Problem

The tragic event of the abolition of graced freedom could be said to symbolize, also and at the same time, the unfortunate turn from the revelatory-covenantal relationship, which is born of grace and based solely on faith, to the advent of a relationship as religion, a pattern in which the movement is now directed from the human to the divine; this is yet another form of bondage cloaked as "liberty" from the oppressive constraints of obedience. Religious pattern, evident as ritual and myth, is now held in the control of the human who will formulate a belief system and concepts of the divine suitable to social, cultural, and spiritual necessities; it is a fully immanent reality, with any transcendent dimension merely a product of imaginative projection on the part of the devotee(s). The striking image of the Tower of Babel is but one of many narrative testimonies to the tragic consequences of the advent of religion as a falsely perceived viable alternative to the revelatory-covenantal relationship established by God, the only environment in which graced freedom can survive and thrive. One's allegiance (and consequent "worship") is given to the religious order and the god it represents, all under the controlling oversight of the priestly order. Religion thus becomes the vehicle for the human expression of a search for "freedom" from the tyranny of worldly realities; the formalized desire to transcend the current and oppressive encounters with finitude in all its limitations; the wish to connect with and placate the god or gods, by virtue of works of virtue, morality, ritualistic practice, and satisfaction of imposed spiritual laws. We will return to this subject, and more fully, in a later chapter.

We would be remiss not to mention the singularly crucial act of God in this Genesis account, which foreshadows the extreme cost to the Lord in covering the shame of sin and, as an act of absolute grace and mercy, sacrificing the life of another in order to cover human shame: The Lord God made garments of skin for Adam and his wife, and clothed them (Gen. 3:21)! We must not underestimate the severity of pain this singular act of sacrifice inflicted on the heart of God; even so, God's love and grace alone will cover the shame of sin that we humans inflict upon ourselves in such acts of disobedience and assertions of false or foolish pride. Time and again, throughout the long and often perverted history of humankind as God's covenant partner, it is the Lord who will take (and takes) the initiative to wrap *anthropos* in the garments of grace. It strikes one's theological sensibility that whenever Adam and Eve beheld the very garments with which they were clothed by God, they would remember the life sacrificed to cover their sin shame; perhaps one could suggest a parallel to the New Testament image of the risen Christ bearing the marks of his passion on his glorified body (see John 20:20–29), which could also be understood as a reminder to the one who has put on (or is clothed in) Christ of the sacrifice made for redemption from sin.

Having been banished from the "Garden" in which graced freedom was the sum and substance of the order of life and covenantal community, *anthropos* is now to serve the very substance from which he had been formed by the hand of the living God; no longer can he relish in graced freedom, now Adam serves—as do both Eve and the serpent—under the judgment they have not so much received as brought on themselves through the surrender of graced freedom. As a consequence there will be an ongoing struggle between the embrace of graced freedom and the obedience of faithfulness to the full intent of God for the life of his covenant partner, and the propensity to surrender oneself to that slavery which is sin and submission to a bondage that cannot so easily be escaped or broken; one can only be released from these chains of captivity by the hammer forever held in the hands of a gracious God alone! Yet God *is* gracious and the continuing narrative of God's interactions with Noah, Abraham, Isaac, Jacob, and the host of Israel's children and historical covenant community—up to and including the greatest of Israel's liberators, Moses—is one in which we witness grace in the steadfastness of the Lord's love as God seeks, again and again, to re-establish graced freedom as the fundamental-ontological reality of his people and the world—his creation.

Before moving forward in this great drama of God and Israel as a people, we want to remember that we are tracing the contours of the evangelical testimony to graced freedom, which is the substance of the theological narrative itself, bearing definitive witness to the reality of graced freedom as that ontological reality with origins in the covenantal characteristic of a loving and generous God. It is just this testimony to evangelical freedom that serves as the foundation of our contention that the concept of freedom *for* humanity is grounded in biblical-theological affirmations and convictions.

We are tracing these contours of biblical and theological witness to establish the basis for the assertion that—as heir to this same biblical testimony to graced freedom—the *communio sanctorum* in North America holds great potential for ethical impact worldwide in addressing any/all situations in which the dignity of humanity is compromised, and to provide valuable and motivational insights in advancing the reclamation of graced freedom as a divinely established order. The meaning of salvation can only be fully understood and appreciated when one acknowledges that graced freedom is central to the biblical concept of salvation; we are not saved for the enhancement of self-expression as a personal liberty, rather, we are saved so that we might, by virtue of the Holy Spirit, be motivated by graced freedom (as ontological transformation), as the sole basis for obedience to and worship of the one true God. In turn such graced freedom becomes the basis for the enrichment and enlargement of the community of faith *in* the world and *for* the world.

2

Israel: Dialectic of Obedience-Disobedience

"A new king, who had not known Joseph, came to power in Egypt."
—Exodus 1:8

THE PHRASE ABOVE OPENS one of the most important narratives in the Old Testament, as a prelude to the redemption of the Hebrews (i.e., a "mixed people") from bondage in Egypt. The story of the exodus from Egypt is, of course, prefaced with those wonderful narrative accounts of the patriarchs of Israel—Abraham, Isaac, and Jacob—ending as they do with the death of Joseph in Egypt and the rise of the pharaoh who had no knowledge of the importance of Joseph in the history of pharaoh's own people. We could trace the lineage of graced freedom throughout the entirety of the patriarchal accounts, but it would extend this essay beyond reason (and perhaps even try the patience of the reader). Nevertheless, the story of the patriarchs is vital background to the foundation of the covenantal relationship between God and his people; we assume the reader has prior knowledge of this essential history; if not, he or she is encouraged to read (or re-read) those central narratives as a prelude to this chapter of our study in graced freedom. What must be affirmed in relation to the patriarchs is that they did not receive the call of Yahweh to freedom *from* only, but also to freedom *for* covenantal obedience and worship of the one true God. This same truth is the basis of our introduction to this portion of our study; an affirmation from the Book

Israel: Dialectic of Obedience-Disobedience

of Exodus is essential to our continued exploration and purpose: "The Israelites groaned because of their difficult labor, and they cried out; and their cry for help ascended to God because of the difficult labor. So God heard their groaning, and He remembered His covenant with Abraham, Isaac, and Jacob. God saw the Israelites, and He took notice" (Exod. 2:23b–25).

The assertion that God heard (the) groaning of Israel in slavery and remembered His covenant with the patriarchs makes an immediate historical connection between where Israel suffered in her present plight and the covenantal relationship God had established with their ancestors as the basis for the compassionate response of God to their current crisis and cry for help. This passage also implies certain attentiveness on the part of God to the historical realities of his people, to the degree that even their groaning would not escape the attention of God; the same degree of attentiveness is captured even more graphically in the acknowledgement that God saw the Israelites, and He took notice. The vigilance of God (as in God saw) is surpassed in significance only by the term (knew), which implies a form of intimacy as well as immediacy; the covenantal relationship could, and certainly would, be violated by the human partner, but would never be dishonored by the Lord God, who would remain both loyal and faithful to the promises made to the patriarchs in the establishment and maintenance of a graced freedom for his people.

For our present purposes we pick up the narrative with the account of the flight of Moses from Egypt, after having murdered an Egyptian guard, his subsequent association with Jethro, the priest of Midian, and the dramatic encounter with Yahweh, the God of Israel.

> Meanwhile, Moses was shepherding the flock of his father-in-law Jethro, the priest of Midian. He led the flock to the far side of the wilderness and came to Horeb, the mountain of God. Then the angel of the Lord appeared to him in a flame of fire within a bush. As Moses looked, he saw that the bush was on fire but was not consumed. So Moses thought: I must go over and look at this remarkable sight. Why isn't the bush burning up? When the Lord saw that he had gone over to look, God called out to him from the bush, "Moses, Moses!" "Here I am," he answered. "Do not come closer," He said. "Remove the sandals from your feet, for the place where you are standing is holy ground." Then He continued, "I am the God of your father, the God of Abraham, the God of Isaac, and the God of Jacob." Moses hid his face because he was afraid to look at God. (Exod. 3:1–6)

A Pastoral Proposal for an Evangelical Theology of Freedom

The Hebrew raised in the palace of Pharaoh, this renegade/fugitive from the land of Egypt, is chosen of God—the God of his "father"—to become the "liberator" of the children of Israel whose cries have been heard by the only God to make genuine freedom a reality; but as we will soon discover, such freedom, while manifest in liberation from hard labor and injustice in Egypt, is fundamentally the graced freedom for obedience to and worship of this covenantal God of Abraham, Isaac, and Jacob. In this revelation Moses witnesses the glory of God, which can only be responded to appropriately with awe and reverence; the mention of this site being "holy ground" also strengthens the claim to the encounter with this God as nothing less than a worshipful event demanding immediate and unquestioned obedience to the command issued (i.e., "Do not come near; take the sandals off your feet. . . ."). Attentiveness to the voice of the Lord God is preceded by acknowledgment of the encounter with the Holy Other who is nonetheless present with, to, and for his people in their distress. The first manifestation of the absolute freedom of the God who confers graced freedom is evident in the words that follow:

> Then the Lord said, "I have observed the misery of My people in Egypt, and have heard them crying out because of their oppressors, and I know about their sufferings. I have come down to rescue them from the power of the Egyptians and to bring them from that land to a good and spacious land, a land flowing with milk and honey. . . . The Israelites cry for help has come to Me, and I have seen the way the Egyptians are oppressing them. Therefore, go. I am sending you to Pharaoh so that you may lead my people, the Israelites, out of Egypt." (Exod. 3:7–10)

This is far more than mere literary redundancy of that which has already been affirmed concerning the Lord God in the earlier portions of the narrative; this segment of the story adds dramatic effect in the expressed intentions of God as pathos for the sufferings of his people, a pathos also evident as the first word of promise implicit in the mention of a good and broad land, a land flowing with milk and honey. In the bestowal of graced freedom God does not simply lift the lock of oppression's chains or bring about a concise victory over the forces that hold Israel in bondage; God also continues to guide his people in the direction of the fulfillment of the covenantal promise to Abraham, Isaac, and Jacob. But with the gift of the land and the bestowal of graced freedom will come obligatory obedience to the will and way of Yahweh, who, as Israel will learn in the wilderness

Israel: Dialectic of Obedience-Disobedience

wandering is a jealous God; devotion to and worship of the one true God holds no room for compromise, as graced freedom is given for the purposes of obedience. This is not to be seen, however, as but another form of slavery or oppression, as the obedience implied in graced freedom is both freedom from and for; that is to say, freedom from all that is genuinely unfulfilling and merely brings about servitude in some form or other, and freedom for genuine fulfillment and graced existence in worship of and service to the one true God whose faithfulness (*hesed*) is evident in the depth of his pathos and his covenantal love for his people.

Anyone familiar with this account knows how, in response to the query of Moses as to the specific "name" of this God he has encountered, God said to Moses, "I AM WHO I AM. This is what you are to say to the Israelites, I AM has sent me to you. God also said to Moses, "Say this to the Israelites, 'Yahweh, the God of your fathers, the God of Abraham, the God of Isaac, and the God of Jacob, has sent me to you." This is My name forever, and this is how I am to be remembered in every generation" (Exod. 3:14–15). God affirms that he will not be a god of religion—one to be cajoled and manipulated by devotees—but he is the God of absolute freedom (expressed in the phrase "I AM WHO I AM," (or as in other translations, "I WILL BE WHO I WILL BE"), the God who is and who will be according to his own being; as the God of absolute freedom he will provide graced freedom for all who enter his revelatory-covenantal relationship of graced freedom; obedience will not be coerced any more than loving devotion to this God (YAHWEH) would be genuine or acceptable if coerced.

Moses was instructed to inform the people of Israel that this is no mere tribal deity, a "god of the mountain or desert," but the same God who dealt graciously with their ancestors—Abraham, Isaac, and Jacob, the Lord who demonstrates his supreme freedom in the establishment and maintenance of the covenant (see Exod. 6:1–5), and in the constancy of loving regard for the people of Israel (i.e., God's *pathos*). This God looks to the formation of intimacy with his people as fundamental to the covenantal relationship to be shared, the graced freedom to be given, and the obedience to be offered in return demonstrated as faith and love. It is not merely liberation from socio-political exploitation that this God enacts (although such liberation is a reality of his gracious intervention on behalf of the Hebrew people in bondage), but freedom to worship, serve, and deepen in devotional commitments to the cause he has established for his covenant people and his created world (see Exod. 8:1). Israel then, as a notion of "liberated" slaves, is to live that graced freedom God has conferred through worship, devotion, and obedience to God's will, serving the Lord God and no other. The point being that Israel will benefit from graced freedom only to the degree that she remains obedient to the Lord God and faithful to her covenantal obligations; anything short of such obedience and faithfulness will plunge this people back into bondage of another kind, but no less severe in its consequences (perhaps, even more severe).

From the first chapters in the Book of Exodus to the closing lines from the book of the prophet Malachi, we witness a community of faith in constant flux, caught between the joy of living in graced freedom and obedience to the bondage and severest of losses (including exile and the destruction of the walls of Jerusalem) as a consequence of her failure to obey and a flirtation with other gods and unacceptable religious rituals of every kind. While it would be rewarding (to say the least) to cover each and all of the prophets (including, of course, the Book of Judges), the brevity of this essay and its purpose prohibit covering this fascinating history; what we will do, instead, is focus on select prophetic writings as representative of the period of the prophets, ending with Malachi as the prelude to the gospels and select epistolary writings. The prophets offer astounding testimony to the purpose of graced freedom and to the history of recurring disobedience on the part of God's people Israel, and the disastrous consequences of such disobedience.

THE VOICE OF ISAIAH

One such prophet is Isaiah who, from his opening words laments the failure of Israel to live responsibly with the graced freedom God had provided:

> Listen, heavens, and pay attention, earth,
> for the LORD has spoken:
> "I have raised children and brought them up,
> but they have rebelled against Me.
> The ox knows its owner
> and the donkey its master's feeding trough;
> but Israel does not know,
> My people do not understand."
> O, sinful nation,
> people weighed down with iniquity,
> brood of evildoers,
> depraved children!

Israel: Dialectic of Obedience-Disobedience

> They have abandoned the LORD,
> they have despised the Holy One of Israel;
> they have turned their backs on Him. (Isa. 1:2–4)

It is the people who have abused the graced freedom God has conferred, sacrificing such freedom on the altar of disobedience, turning its back on God who is both Lord and Savior; there is nothing left of such freedom, until such time as God chooses to bring redemption to Israel and turn her away from such foolishness and captivity to a renewal of the covenant. The word issued by the prophet Isaiah is itself a manifestation of grace, in that the Lord God does not merely wash his hands of this people, but offers them the opportunity for renewal of faith and the reestablishment of graced freedom. Israel was to see obedience to the will of the Lord and the faithful expression of such obedience as extending beyond the normalized ritualistic practice of the Temple; worship is always directed to God, but it is also that affirmation of the covenantal relationship in which the people of God are empowered to enact justice for those who are less fortunate in their midst. Whenever worship as an act of graced freedom is detached from service in the name and to the glory of the Lord, it becomes little more than rote, ritualistic practice, evident in the prophet's declaration on behalf of God:

> "What are all of your sacrifices to Me"?
> asks the LORD.
> "I have had enough of burnt offerings and rams
> and the fat of well-fed cattle;
> I have no desire for the blood of bulls,
>   lambs, or male goats.
> When you come to appear before Me,
> who requires this from you—
> this trampling of my courts?
> Stop bringing useless offerings.
> Your incense is detestable to Me . . .
>   When you lift up your hands in prayer,
> I will refuse to look at you;
> even if you offer countless prayers,
> I will not listen.
> Your hands are covered with blood.
> Wash yourselves. Cleanse yourselves.
> Remove your evil deeds from My sight.
> Stop doing evil.
> Learn to do what is good.

A Pastoral Proposal for an Evangelical Theology of Freedom

> Seek justice.
> Correct the oppressor.
> Defend the rights of the fatherless,
> Plead the widow's cause." (Isa. 1:11–12, 15–17)

There can be no meaningful sense of obedience to the will of God that stops short of concrete actions taken on behalf of those whose lives are dependent on the affirmation of and engagement with what is a just cause in the sight of the Lord; even worship must lead to yet another form of obedience to God, in the pursuit of justice for the less fortunate in the midst of God's people and even to the resident alien. Graced freedom is conferred upon Israel so that she may become a people who serve the Lord in serving those who know only the deprivation of all things needful—just as Israel had experienced the same while slaves in the land of Egypt. We must never forget that worship, as a liturgical event, frames the other forms of obedience to the Lord that extend well beyond the four walls of any one sanctuary; obedience is a lived reality and not merely a posture to be assumed in the presence of the altar on the Sabbath. Graced freedom is evident in both individual believer and the communio sanctorum, whenever and wherever servants of the Lord step into the void of the less fortunate with the gracious gift of compassion, attentiveness to suffering, and the refreshment of restorative care in concrete form. In the passage above we overhear a clear and poignant condemnation of all forms of ritual that are, in fact, a betrayal of graced freedom in that such ritualistic actions lack evidence of genuine obedience as benevolence toward the widow and the orphan. We recall the counsel of Christ who admonished that in bringing one's "gift" to the altar and remembering while kneeling there the brother or sister with whom reconciliation has not been achieved, that worshipper should leave the gift there, and first go and be reconciled, and then return to present the gift. The evidence of genuineness in worship is seen in the reconciliatory act, which is obedience, and therefore a clear manifestation of graced freedom; whereas the simply ritualistic presentation of the "gift" minus such obedience is actually a betrayal of graced freedom.

The ritualistic patterns have taken on the oppressive air of necessity and rote compliance; no longer do these essential rituals, intended to maintain the covenantal relationship, promote the graced freedom associated with their origin. These practices have become a burden on the people and a distraction from the deeper devotion to God and a deliberate desire to pursue God's will, which they were meant to enhance. Even prayer, the

Israel: Dialectic of Obedience-Disobedience

most basic expression of the covenantal relationship, has become void of any semblance of authenticity, to such a degree that the Lord God declares a refusal to honor such prayer. And yet, even in this most deplorable of circumstances, in which the people of Israel have brought upon themselves the displeasure and judgment of the Lord God, there is the promise of the restoration of that same graced freedom forfeited in their disobedience. In words that resonate with an eschatological theme, words that are rich in imagery of redemption and restoration, the prophet proclaims:

> Comfort, comfort my people, says your God. Speak tenderly to Jerusalem, and cry to her that her warfare is ended, that her iniquity is pardoned, that she has received from the Lord's hand double for all her sins. A voice cries: "In the wilderness prepare the way of the Lord; make straight in the desert a highway for our God. Every valet shall be lifted up, and every mountain and hill be made low; the uneven ground shall become level, and the rough places a plain. And the glory of the Lord shall be revealed, and all flesh shall see it together, for the mouth of the Lord has spoken." (Isa. 40:1–5 ESV)

It may not be immediately apparent that this passage constitutes a restoration of what we have called graced freedom. Nevertheless, the promise of return from exile and future restoration implies a reaffirmation of graced freedom and is declared even more forcefully in the following acclamation: "Remember these things, O Jacob, and Israel, for you are my servant; I formed you; you are my servant; O Israel, you will not be forgotten by me. I have blotted out your transgressions like a cloud and your sins like mist; return to me, for I have redeemed you" (Isa. 44:21–22 ESV).

One must not disassociate the redemption announced in this proclamation of Isaiah (i.e., the restoration of graced freedom) from God's provision of the basis, or renewed foundation, for obedience and faithfulness to the covenantal relationship. Israel is not redeemed from the bondage of exile solely for the purposes of socio-political independence; this redemption of the Lord runs much deeper, being that form of divinely conferred freedom that alone makes possible both reconciliation and renewed worship. Recall that Israel was delivered from bondage in Egypt so that the people might worship Yahweh in the wilderness (see Exod. 5).

This point is being stressed because one of the recurring themes throughout the whole of the Old and New Testaments is the one form of freedom that is fundamental to the fulfillment of human life, and that is the graced freedom for the purposes of obedience to the Lord God, an obedience manifest in faithful worship as prayer, praise, sacrifice, and service to the glory of God. When the great St. Augustine affirmed that humans have been created for communion with God and that "our hearts are restless" until they find their rest in God, he was confessing that human life can only find fulfillment in the expression of graced freedom in obedience (as an expression of loving worship) and loving worship (as a manifestation of obedience). Worship of anything other than the Lord God is an obvious violation of graced freedom in treating the penultimate as ultimate; with the worship of the heart misdirected in attention to that which is penultimate, obedience is given to a lie and not to Truth, a lie which results in bondage.

THE VOICE OF JEREMIAH

The interdependence of graced freedom, obedience, worship, and service is one that is truly inextricable, given clarity and profound expression in the writings of the prophet Jeremiah to which we now turn our attention. After the call received from the Lord, as the mouthpiece of God Jeremiah issued this scathing indictment:

> This is what the Lord says:
> What fault did your fathers find in Me
> that they went so far from Me,
> followed worthless idols,
> and became worthless themselves?
> They stopped asking, "Where is the LORD
> who brought us from the land of Egypt,
> who led us through the wilderness,
> through a land of deserts and ravines,
> through a land of drought and darkness,
> a land no one traveled through
> and where no one lived?
> I brought you to a fertile land,
> to eat its fruit and bounty,
> but after you entered, you defiled My land;
> you made My inheritance detestable.
> The priests quit asking, "Where is the LORD?"
> The experts in the law no longer knew Me,
> and the rulers rebelled against Me.
> The prophets prophesied by Baal
> and followed useless idols. (Jer. 2:5–8)

Israel: Dialectic of Obedience-Disobedience

What is striking in this indictment is the manner in which memory, idolatry, and disassociation from Yahweh (e.g., "Where is the Lord?") are forged and disclosed as disobedience; the voice of the prophet (speaking on behalf of the Lord) resonates with pathos for the loss of relationship and the corruption of covenant; the assertion that all have turned to the worship of idols, and to the Baal, implies a form of bondage, since these false gods cannot confer the same graced freedom God had provided for the purposes of obedience and fulfillment of life, which is evident in the language of useless idols, "useless" because they cannot give anything of value to the enrichment of life in faith, but demand a reverence and obedience of their own (or, we should say, are perceived to demand reverence and obedience, since in reality they are deaf, dumb, and illusory). The unilateral dimension of idolatry is a relational absurdity when compared with the intimacy and reciprocal nature of the relationship Yahweh has established and desires with the covenant community.

In a later chapter of the Book of Jeremiah the prophet is himself reminded by Yahweh of the essential nature of the covenantal relationship and how faithfulness and freedom have a foundation in and find expression through obedience:

> This is the word that came to Jeremiah from the Lord: "Listen to the words of this covenant and tell them to the men of Judah and the residents of Jerusalem. You must tell them: This is what the Lord, the God of Israel, says: 'Let a curse be on the man who does not obey the words of this covenant, which I commanded your ancestors when I brought them out of the land of Egypt, out of the iron furnace.' I declared: 'Obey me, and do everything that I commanded you, and you will be My people, and I will be your God,' in order to establish the oath I swore to your ancestors, to give them a land flowing with milk and honey, as it is today." And I answered, "Amen, Lord." (Jer. 11:1–5)

We note with interest the reference, once again, to the exodus from Egypt and the centrality of this singular historical event as an act of covenantal faithfulness on the part of Yahweh, as well as the touchstone of covenantal obedience on the part of God's people. It would appear that the liberation experienced by Israel in the exodus from Egypt was intended to serve as a historical paradigm for that greater graced freedom conferred by the Lord for the purposes of obedience and enrichment of the covenantal relationship shared with his people. There is an association made between

A Pastoral Proposal for an Evangelical Theology of Freedom

the tendency to forget this community-forming event of liberation and indifference vis-à-vis the furtherance of covenantal obligation on the part of Israel. Obedience to the commands of the Lord is concrete evidence of both a healthy communal memory of the reason for the faithfulness owed to Yahweh alone, and genuine gratitude for the conferral of graced freedom as the foundation of such obedience. It is also to be noted how the continuance of the relationship with the Lord is based on obedience to his commands, that is to say, the disuse of graced freedom leading to disobedience also and at the same time injures the relationship with the Lord.

As emissary for the Lord and as the mouthpiece for God's Word, the prophet Jeremiah also issues stern warnings (as do other prophets as well) against both the leaders of Israel (i.e., "shepherds") and those who claim to be "prophets of the Lord." In the twenty-third chapter of Jeremiah when speaking on behalf of Yahweh, the prophet admonishes Israel's leaders:

> "Woe to the shepherds who destroy and scatter the sheep of My pasture!" [This is] the Lord's declaration. "Therefore, this is what the Lord, the God of Israel, says about the shepherds who shepherd My people: You have scattered My flock, banished them, and have not attended to them. I will attend to you because of your evil acts"—the Lord's declaration. "I will gather the remnant of My flock from all the lands where I have banished them, and I will return them to their grazing land. They will become numerous. I will raise up shepherds over them who will shepherd them. They will no longer be afraid or dismayed, nor will any be missing." [This is] the Lord's declaration. (Jer. 23:1–4)

The leaders ("shepherds") of Israel were placed in their positions (one could say, gifted with their respective offices as act of God's grace) to serve the Lord by serving God's people (the "flock" of the Lord); they were given graced freedom so that they might rule from within a relationship of obedience to the will of God for Israel (the "sheep" of God's fold). It would appear from the record of Jeremiah that the "shepherds" turned aside from obedience, forfeiting graced freedom, becoming enslaved to the spirit of greed, self-enrichment, and injustice at the expense of the enrichment of God's people, that is, their disobedience resulted in the "scattering" of the "flock" of Yahweh. Rather than reflect the same covenant commitment witnessed in the historical actions of Yahweh, actions that disclosed the Lord's freedom, compassion, justice, and regard for the communal as well as the individual welfare of the "flock," these "shepherds" took it upon themselves to

Israel: Dialectic of Obedience-Disobedience

treat God's people with complete disregard, forsaking faithfulness to their respective responsibilities as "shepherds" and forsaking graced freedom for slavery to sinful disobedience.

In response to the disobedience, rebellion, and disregard of these "shepherds" the Lord declares that he will now "raise up" shepherds who will obey the will of the Lord and therefore demonstrate the superior power of graced freedom in service that will enrich the lives of God's people and enlarge the community of faith. In fact, in the passages to follow the recapitulation of that form of liberation first revealed in the exodus from Egypt (therefore a new paradigm for freedom) is announced as the will of the Lord, and it is asserted that this event will become the new "gospel" of freedom and reunion: "'The days are coming'—the Lord's declaration—'when it will no longer be said: As the Lord lives who brought the Israelites from the land of Egypt, but: As the Lord lives, who brought and led the descendants of the house of Israel from the land of the north and from all other countries where I had banished them. They will dwell once more in their own land'" (Jer. 23:7–8).

Several characteristics of this passage are to be noted in particular. One is that there will now be a new reference point for the historical remembrance of the people of God, an event which will replicate the exodus from Egypt in terms of its disclosive character of how historical events of liberation (as a consequence of God's gracious action[s]) resound with the restoration of graced freedom as emblematic of reconciliation. Also, there is a direct relationship made between the alienation of having been "banished," as a consequence of disobedience and therefore the overt rejection of graced freedom, and the return to "their own land" as the concrete manifestation of God's merciful forgiveness and restoration of graced freedom as the "new" beginning, or renewal of covenantal relationship. Finally, there is the assertion that this is purely the act of God and therefore a denial of the human capacity to break the bondage of disobedience and sin once graced freedom has been surrendered; graced freedom can only be conferred (or even recapitulated) by God as the source of all true freedom to obey, and in obedience to discover the enlargement and enrichment of life in faith for the individual and community. This passage also annunciates, with such profound clarity of vision, just how it is that the dialectic of obedience-disobedience in Israel does not distract Yahweh from the fulfillment of his purposes for his people as a reflection of God's desire for the whole of the world—a fulfillment that will be (as proleptic) disclosed in Jesus

A Pastoral Proposal for an Evangelical Theology of Freedom

Christ—and the extent to which graced freedom is fundamental to that same fulfillment (which we will visit again in our study of Revelation).

The sharpness of the dialectic (obedience-disobedience) and the consequences of the same extend as well to those nations (and in Jeremiah, Assyria and Babylon in particular) that would take advantage of Israel in her weakness and vulnerability; Yahweh will not tolerate injustice in the nations of world, even when they are used as an instrument of his divine judgment. While one cannot assert with any certainty at all that graced freedom is reserved to the children of covenant, it can be said that there is a kind of (graced) freedom in all forms of governance (then and now) that comes with accountability to God for just and equitable treatment of one's citizens, subjects, and so on. To that degree the misuse of such freedom places those who govern under the shadow of God's wrath, whenever they (then and now) fail to remain faithful (read: obedient) to God's will for those who assume/hold such office of governance. This is clearly stated in one of the closing declarations of the prophet Jeremiah:

> Israel is a stray lamb,
> chased by lions.
> The first who devoured him was
> the king of Assyria;
> this last who crushed
> his bones
> was Nebuchadnezzar
> king of Babylon.
> Therefore, this is what the LORD
> of Hosts, the God of Israel, says:
> "I am about to punish the king of Babylon
> for his land just as I punished the king
> of Assyria.
> I will return Israel
> to his grazing land,
> and he will feed on Carmel
> and Bashan;
> he will be satisfied
> in the hill country of Ephraim
> and of Gilead.
> In those days and at that time—
> [this is]
> the LORD's declaration—
> one will search for Israel's guilt,
> but there will be none,

and for Judah's sins,
but they will not be found,
for I will forgive those I leave
as a remnant. (Jer. 50:17–20)

The liberation of Israel and Judah from the bondage they have endured is disclosive of the forgiveness of God and the reestablishment of graced freedom as the basis of a new obedience in the renewal of the covenantal relationship—a relationship of recapitulated faith evident in the absence of both "guilt" and "sins." Once again there is the re-assertion of a re-turn to the "land" (note the reference to "grazing" land) on which the people will not only settle once again, but feed upon the nurturing obedience of graced freedom in a renewed relationship with the Lord God. This reference to "land" is also vital because of its association with "place;" the reality of graced freedom is the correlate of "land" since freedom expressed must be within the very real context of a "place" that is individuated in terms of communal identity and a sense of well-being among those seeking to faithfully obey the commandments of God. Israel's sense of what constitutes obedience to the Lord God cannot be divorced from their association with the "land" as their own unique "place" for the expression of the graced freedom as the basis for such obedience, which is why the exilic experience was such a powerful materialization of the great cost of disobedience as both the loss of freedom and disinheritance of the "land;" in connection with this concept recall the excruciatingly painful words of Psalm 137, and in particular these: "How can we sing the Lord's song on foreign soil?" (Ps. 137:4).

OTHER PROPHETIC VOICES

In an essay of such brevity as this, we cannot possibly do justice to each of the prophetic utterances in the canonical writings from Hosea to Malachi, it is important however that we dip in here and there, in order to uncover passages that are paradigmatic of these critically important prophetic voices and instructive for our theme in this essay. Even though we must once again be selective, the choices are representative of the central significance of each prophetic voice we have elected as illustrative of the covenantal dynamic of the dialectical obedience-disobedience, of graced freedom, and bondage of sin which is consequence of the forfeiture of graced freedom.

A Pastoral Proposal for an Evangelical Theology of Freedom

One of the prevailing images used in the prophetic utterances of the prophet Hosea is that of the unfaithful spouse as a symbol of the infidelity of Israel in their covenantal relationship with the Lord:

> When the Lord first spoke to Hosea, He said this to him:
> Go and marry
> a promiscuous wife
> and have children
> of promiscuity,
> for the whole land
> has been promiscuous
> by abandoning the Lord. (Hos. 1:2)

Of course the prophet is obedient and does as the Lord has commanded, giving testimony to the people of God that their turn to idols and unfaithfulness to God's covenant has (as in Genesis) also brought a curse to the "land." And again in the fourth chapter we overhear the condemnation of the Lord as God's case against Israel for their unfaithfulness and disobedience:

> Hear the word of the Lord,
> people of Israel,
> for the LORD has a case
> against the inhabitants
> of the land:
> There is no truth,
> no faithful love,
> and no knowledge of God
> in the land!
> Cursing, lying,
> murder, stealing,
> and adultery are rampant;
> one act of bloodshed
> follows another.
> For this reason the land mourns,
> and everyone who lives
> in it languishes,
> along with wild animals
> and birds of the sky;
> even the fish
> of the sea disappear. (Hos. 4:1–3)

Israel: Dialectic of Obedience-Disobedience

This propensity to forfeit graced freedom in the pursuit of sinful self-assertions is shown to have dire consequences—or at the very least adverse affects!—on the realm of nature, the whole of the land and sea; once again demonstrating the cosmic effects of disobedience, extending well beyond the boundaries of Israel as land and people. The obvious relevance for our current global environmental crises need not be drawn out here, as we will address this and other relevancies of the forfeiture of graced freedom in a concluding chapter of this essay. For the present we simply stress the wider impact of the forfeiture of graced freedom, which can be held in contrast to the recreation and renewal of all things in the reassertion (actually the faithful embrace) of graced freedom following the necessary repentance and forgiveness. The contemporary tendency to restrict the consequences of sinful disregard for the imperative of obedience to the Lord God to that of the individual and his or her life is overturned, dramatically, in the prophetic affirmation of the forfeiture of graced freedom as adversely affecting life on communal and cosmic levels, as well as the personal.

The prophetic admonition, in its several forms and varieties of historical context is, nevertheless, also a word of encouragement to Israel that in obedience she will discover the enlargement of that graced freedom with which she has been blessed by the Lord God, and in this enlargement and enrichment will, also and at the same time, testify to the surrounding nations how it is that the endemic forms of religious practice are, in reality, a form of bondage and diminishment of life as the Lord God intends for creature and creation. The "gospel" is embedded in this prophetic word of encouragement, as it is in the prophetic word of admonition, because it is the only genuine message of "good news" in the reality of God's proffered graced freedom and obedience as the fulfillment of human life in each and every form of culture and society—beginning, of course with Israel as witness (see Ps. 96: 5, 7–10a and Zech. 8:20–23). When we turn in this essay to the evangelical witness of the New Testament we will hear and see the same, only as the proleptic fulfillment made manifest in Christ and the early Christian community, as in Christianity itself.

For now, we return to the voice of the prophet Hosea. The word of restoration comes in the fourteenth chapter of Hosea, following a call to repentance:

> Israel, return to the Lord
> your God,
> for you have stumbled

A Pastoral Proposal for an Evangelical Theology of Freedom

> in your sin.
> Take words of repentance
> with you
> and return to the LORD.
> Say to Him: "Forgive all [our] sin
> and accept what is good
> so that we may repay You
> with praise from our lips.

The Lord now speaks through the voice of Hosea a word that is incomparable in both the grandeur of the grace stated and the breadth of the promise made:

> I will heal their apostasy;
> I will freely love them,
> for My anger will have turned
> from him.
> I will be like dew
> to Israel;
> he will blossom like the lily
> and take root like
> the cedars of Lebanon.
> His new branches will spread,
> and his splendor will be
> like the olive tree,
> his fragrance, like
> [the forest of] Lebanon.
> The people will return and live
> beneath his shade.
> They will grow grain
> and blossom like the vine.

Once again the language of restoration is couched in terms that allude to the fruitfulness of Israel, which is also associated with the "land" as the sacred place of renewal; the reference to "grain" and "vine," while for many Christians will bring to mind the sacrament of the eucharist, is most likely in the present context (and like the sacrament itself) to be associated with the celebratory joy of reconciliation, return, and reunion, as a proleptic of eschatological realities. Even though there is no one overt reference to graced freedom, the image of the Lord God as "dew" implies both a new day (the "dew" of a new morning) and the gentle refreshment that brings with it the nourishment essential to growth; there can be no such growth and enrichment of life where there is an absence of graced freedom, as

Israel: Dialectic of Obedience-Disobedience

such freedom is the ground (the cultivated soil) in which spiritual rebirth, growth and enrichment are possible.

In the book of the prophet Joel we discover similar themes of judgment due to the idolatry, disobedience, and false worship of the people as is found throughout the prophetic field; the exception in Joel's admonition is his inclusion of the priestly order and the reiteration of the cry to "Blow the trumpet in Zion," an apparent allusion to the sound of the "shophar," used to summon pilgrims to the Temple for any number of annual observances, but here referring to the need for fasting and repentance. Joel warns of the "day of the Lord" as one of judgment and a call to accountability; but it is also a day of restoration and renewal:

> Great is the day of the Lord and terrible,
> who can endure it?
> And yet, the LORD says, even now
> turn back to me with your whole heart,
> fast, and weep, and beat your breasts.
> Rend your hearts and not your garments;
> turn back to the LORD your God;
> for he is gracious and compassionate,
> long suffering and ever constant,
> always ready to repent of the threatened evil.
> It may be he will turn back and repent
> and leave a blessing behind him,
> blessing enough for grain-offering and drink-offering
> for the Lord your God. (Joel 2:11b–14 NEB)

The necessity for repentance beyond the ceremonial is evident in the word of the Lord that the people will now need to "[r]end (their) hearts and not (their) garments." The anguish of the repentant heart would be evident in the capacity and willingness to "turn back" to the Lord God and in such repentant action to once again reach out to embrace the graced freedom of obedience in the establishment of a renewed relationship of faith and devotion to the will and way of God. The prophet points to the grace, compassion, and long suffering of the Lord as the basis of any hope that the covenantal relationship can be restored; just as the relinquishing of graced freedom is the precedent for sinful disobedience and subsequent bondage, so repentance is the precedent of hope for the conferral or restoration of graced freedom, and can only be realized because the Lord God is gracious and compassionate, remaining constant in faithfulness to the covenant he established with Abraham, Isaac, and Jacob; as Joel expresses the same truth: "The Lord's love burned with zeal for his land, and he was moved with compassion for his people" (Joel 2:18 NEB).

Before turning our attention to the New Testament, we will consider one other paradigmatic prophetic book, and that is the Book of Micah. One of the muscular characteristics of the pronouncements of this prophet is his focus on the social dynamic of disobedience which is, like any other form of disobedience, a form of bondage to the sinner, but also creates an environment of oppression and bondage for others:

> Shame on those who lie in bed planning evil and wicked deeds
> and rise at daybreak to do them,
> knowing that they have the power!
> They covet land and take it by force;
> if they want a house, they seize it;
> they rob a man of his home
> and steal every man's inheritance.
> Therefore these are the words of the Lord:
> Listen, for this whole brood I am planning disaster,
> whose yoke you cannot shake from your necks
> and walk upright; it shall be your hour of disaster.
> (Micah 2:1–3 NEB)

There is an obvious element of historical (and covenantal) amnesia in this disobedience, where those who plan and carry out such "evil" have disregarded the constant refrain that they—as Israel—are to treat others with justice and mercy, just as they had been treated by the Lord God in their liberation from bondage in Egypt (remembering that there is no discontinuity between the covenantal identity of any one generation of Israel and another; that is, the exodus event is not merely a historical memory, but was also understood as contemporaneous with each generation celebrating Passover). The more they crave in their depraved indifference, the greater the degree of bondage/captivity to sin and sinful disregard for the will of the Lord; the peace of a restful night has been overtaken by the mounting desire to have more power, which creates the illusion of independence and self-sufficiency.

Yet, despite the disobedience and consequent injustice, despite the entrenched sinfulness of the leaders and people, despite the historical occurrences of God's judgment on Israel, there remains the word of promise and hope. A promise and hope that is based solely on the mercy and steadfast love of the ever-faithful Lord, applied to the people whose disobedience will one day be turned to devotion once again in the constant refrain of the dialectic of obedience-disobedience. It is the covenantal love and faithfulness of the Lord that leads to the future restoration of graced freedom and fulfillment of life:

> Who is a God like You,
> removing iniquity and passing
> over rebellion
> for the remnant
> of His inheritance?
> He does not hold on
> to His anger forever,
> because He delights
> in faithful love.
> He will again have compassion
> on us;
> He will vanquish
> our iniquities.
> You will cast all our sins
> into the depths of the sea.
> You will show loyalty to Jacob
> and faithful love to Abraham,
> as You swore to our fathers
> from days long ago. (Micah 7:18–20)

We cannot overlook either the reference to the "fathers" of the covenant (as represented by Jacob and Abraham) or the finality of the forgiveness of the Lord as the ground upon which the reality of graced freedom is to be restored. The conclusion of the prophetic voice on this gracious word from the Lord affirms God's desire to establish and restore graced freedom as the bedrock of the life promised in covenantal communion, with such freedom making loving obedience possible. God is not dissuaded by the dialectic of obedience-disobedience, as God's faithfulness to the covenant of promise is grounded in his being a God of freedom, steadfast love, justice, faithfulness, and fulfillment; the means to all that God desires for his covenant community is graced freedom, which is also and always the gift of God. The steadfast love of the Lord is a manifestation of God's eternal freedom, making love essential to graced freedom and to any expression of obedience; to be genuine, the obedience the Lord desires cannot be coerced, it must come as a manifestation of love for the Lord and the loving desire to do God's will.

A Pastoral Proposal for an Evangelical Theology of Freedom

Throughout the literature of the prophets there is the voiced concern not only with the idolatrous practices of Israel, practices learned from surrounding religions, but with the degree of injustice and evident disobedience to the will and ways God has commanded of the covenant partner; and all of this condemnation is driven by God's desire to see the children of Israel return to the form of graced freedom that has been discarded in the actions of disobedience, which has not resulted in even greater liberty or freedom, but rather in bondage and brokenness with and within the whole of the covenant community. Of course there is also and at the same time the prevailing theme of the "remnant," those who have not "bent the knee to Baal," having remained faithful and committed to the claims of the Lord on their lives as an essential characteristic of the covenant. That which distinguishes Israel from all of the surrounding cultures is not merely the practice of a particular form of religious ritual—although there is a significant difference between the purpose behind the sacrifices commanded by Yahweh and those of the pagan religions. Israel is fundamentally distinguished from all other cultures by virtue of the fact that she is in covenant with Yahweh, in that the whole of her existence is to be driven by devotion to the Lord and faithfulness to the covenantal commitments, in that she has been blessed to receive graced freedom for obedience and in such obedience to discover the enlargement of life as God intended from the foundation of the world.

Obedience to the commands, both explicit and implicit, of the covenant can only be genuine obedience when it is driven by that form of love embedded in graced freedom, a love that is in response to the multitude of blessings received from the Lord God; both the individual and community of faith are moved by this love and express such love as only graced freedom makes possible. The people of God are set apart from the surrounding cultures and social settings in that they move within the framework of a transcendent reality, a graced freedom afforded them in covenantal love; the bond forged in such freedom is sustained in the constancy of faithfulness and obedience to the Lord God. The dialectic of obedience-disobedience we have undertaken to elaborate in this chapter can only thwart the intent of the Lord to lead the people into a full and productive future; it is in the faithfulness of God that the offer of forgiveness is given as the foundation of reconciliation and restoration of graced freedom. The prophetic pronouncement of both the judgment of God on all forms of disobedience and the promise of forgiveness and reconciliation find clear resonance in the early chapters of all of the Gospels, in particular with the advent of John the Baptist, in the fullness of the teaching of Jesus Christ as in his person and work, and in the elaboration of the proclamation of gospel of grace in the epistles. Graced freedom comes to the apex of its expression with the Incarnation, the proleptic disclosure of the coming "kingdom of God," and the birth of the Christian *communio sanctorum*.

It is only fitting then that we close this chapter and anticipate the next with the words of the prophet Malachi: "Remember the instructions of Moses My Servant, the statutes and ordinances I commanded him at Horeb for all Israel. Look, I am going to send you Elijah the prophet before the great and awesome Day of the Lord comes. And he will turn the hearts of fathers to [their] children and the hearts of children to their fathers" (Mal. 4:4–6a).

3

The New Testament Witness to Graced Freedom

"Here begins the Gospel of Jesus Christ the Son of God. In the prophet Isaiah it stands written: 'Here is my herald whom I send on ahead of you, and he will prepare your way. A voice crying aloud in the wilderness, "Prepare a way for the Lord; clear a straight path for him."' And so it was that John the Baptist appeared in the wilderness proclaiming a baptism in token of repentance, for the forgiveness of sins; and they flocked to him from the whole Judaean country-side and the city of Jerusalem, and were baptized by him in the River Jordan, confessing their sins."

—Mark 1:1–5 NEB

"In the sixth month the angel Gabriel was sent from God to a town in Galilee called Nazareth, with a message for a girl betrothed to a man named Joseph, a descendant of David; the girl's name was Mary."

—Luke 1:26–27 NEB

The openings of the gospels of Mark and Luke set the stage for the focus of this chapter on both John and Baptist and Mary the mother of our Lord as paradigmatic of what we are calling "graced freedom;" that form

The New Testament Witness to Graced Freedom

of freedom which comes from God as a gift and is foundational for free obedience in faith. While we will take up select writings of the apostle Paul in the next chapter (and other epistolary examples as well), and while it is clear that all of the epistles together constitute a particular form of gospel communication in the broader category of "New Testament Literature," the use of "New Testament Witness" in the title of the current chapter is intended to emphasize the roles of John the Baptist and Mary as representative of the new testament (i.e., new covenant) community. While the old and new covenants are distinct, they must not be seen to be unrelated; in the same fashion, while John the Baptist and Mary are employed as truly representative of graced freedom within the new covenant, they must not be considered in any fashion as divorced from those expressions of graced freedom we have already explored in previous chapters, as old covenant realities remained essential to Jewish identity.

Both John and Mary are held to be exemplary of graced freedom in an anticipatory context, where messianic expectation is arguably an unfolding revelation; to that extent both John the Baptist and Mary serve a proleptic capacity in relation to the much broader category of "discipleship," or better said, serve to symbolize a nascent form of free obedience, which will be further developed in the writings of Paul and other epistolary authors as well, to be given further consideration in subsequent chapters. Whereas John the Baptist is the tie to the Old Testament prophetic tradition and the old covenant, representing a form of graced freedom that resonates with the thematic of old covenant free obedience, Mary is the tie to the New Testament and representative of the form of graced freedom that is characteristically associated with proleptic promise of messianic fulfillment, and the faith essential to all expressions of free obedience for those who will become members of the new covenant community. We will not treat the relevant narrative materials in relation to John and Mary as though they were merely mythic, without essential connection to historical necessities and realities; rather, our interest will be in the way such narratives serve to disclose the drama of graced freedom as it unfolds in the New Testament and therefore, primarily, for the *communio sanctorum*.

JOHN THE BAPTIST

Of course our introduction to John the Baptist is through the dramatic re-presentation of the pre-natal experiences of his father and mother—Zechariah and Elizabeth—who are patterned after similar characters in the covenantal narratives of the Old Testament (one thinks immediately of Abraham and Sarah). We needn't rehearse the entire narrative, except to draw attention to the fact that, like Abraham and Sarah, this couple was also elderly (well past the years of child-bearing age) and Elizabeth was said to be barren. Perhaps the theological intent is to draw this striking parallel between the two historically significant couples, but is it also allows for an interpretation of this event (i.e., the conception of John) as an act of God, although conspicuously dissimilar from that the conception of Jesus in the womb of Mary!

It seems essential to the author's intention to narrate how word of this child's conception was brought to Zechariah by the angel, Gabriel, that is, while he is performing his service in the Temple; while the miracle is not (as with the conception of Jesus) a virginal conception, it is, nonetheless, an event of God's direct intervention. This dramatic disclosure resonates with a similar spiritual experience with the two characters who are central to associations with the old covenant (Abraham and Sarah), yet also fulfills the purpose of establishing both the lineage of John (as one who is within the lineage of the priestly/Temple heritage) and the role he will play (prophetically, as in the association with Elijah mentioned in 1:17) as the forerunner of the proclaimed Christ. Each and all of the allusions to the Old Testament covenantal realties serve to strengthen the ties with what will become New Testament covenantal actualities, making it impossible to separate the latter from the former without threatening to snap off the theological thread essential to maintenance of continuity in the presentation of salvation history. In order to understand and appreciate the continuity of God's provision of graced freedom as essential to free obedience in covenantal faith, this affirmation of permanence in the unfolding salvific plan of God is vital!

However, as essential as is this maintenance of continuity, John the Baptist represents more than a symbolic bond with Old Testament covenantal verities; John also holds the indispensable prophetic office as both herald of the coming Messiah, and as the one whose ministry is vital to obligatory preparations for the arrival of the Messiah on the stage of salvation history. While Mark's narrative portrays John as having preached or proclaimed a baptism "of repentance, for the forgiveness of sins" (Mark 1:4), the gospel of St. Luke discloses John's ministry to have also been one of ethical or moral exhortation and guidance, in those actions demonstrative

The New Testament Witness to Graced Freedom

of the repentant heart and soul—of a life lived in free obedience to the will of God:

The people asked (John), "Then what are we to do?" He replied, "The man with two shirts must share with him who has none, and anyone who has food must do the same." Among those who came to be baptized were tax gatherers, and they said to him, "Master, what are we to do?" He told them, "Exact no more than the assessment." Soldiers on service also asked him, "And what of us?" To them he said, "No bullying; no blackmail; make do with your pay!" (Luke 3:10–14 NEB)

The ethical edge to these pronouncements is evident; equally apparent is the resonance with the pronouncements of many—if not most—of the Old Testament prophets, to a people who had strayed from the justice God demanded on behalf of those who were less fortunate and lacking in the basic necessities of life. Those familiar with the "theology" of Luke's gospel will not be surprised at this focus on the centrality of compassion and care given to the less fortunate, as indicative of repentance and obedience, even in the only didactic "preaching" we hear from John.

The need to "do" follows the event of a baptism "of repentance, for the forgiveness of sins," which implies that the capacity to "obey" can only come as the result of the gift of graced freedom through John's baptism, and as indicative or demonstrative of free obedience; one cannot possibly expect those still in bondage to "sin" to have any desire or spiritual faculty whatsoever to fulfill the critically ethical mandates John has annunciated in his "preaching."

We should also note how John's lifestyle: even if John is understood as a "student" of the Essence community (with its early monastic characteristics), this is not merely a dress and dietary habit that marks him as a prophet. John's life style is itself demonstrative of the necessity to detach one's self from anything that would deliberately prohibit free and complete submission to the will and way of God. The free obedience of graced freedom is liable to obstruction and inhibition from a wide variety, or forms, of bondage, for example, materialistic, psychological, socio-political, or spiritual in nature. John's evident "detachment" from "the world" is not a manifestation of early "Manichaeism," or a distain for all things "worldly," so much as it is representative of his complete, total submission of the whole of his life to the service of God in free obedience, as both the "preacher" of a "baptism of repentance, for the forgiveness of sins," and as the one whose "mission" is to prepared the way for the coming of the Messiah. Said differently, John's evident "freedom" to serve is unquestionably a direct result of his complete submission to the will and desire of God for his life; this is primarily an affirmation of genuine obedience as free obedience, in which one seeks to remain faithful to the prior and perceived purpose of the Lord for his/her life; John gives his obedience freely as a recipient of a much more precious gift of grace and the promise of the even greater grace about to be realized as the Messiah steps onto the stage of human history. Grace does not follow faith and obedience, but is also the precedent for both—and in particular because God desires free obedience, as much as God does a love that is freely given!

Taking a closer inspection of John's ethical admonitions to candidates for his "baptism of repentance, for the forgiveness of sins," each of the statements presupposes an awareness of the divine mandate for such just behavior, and the protracted history of covenantal obligations associated with such socio-ethical and community solidifying actions on behalf of those who genuinely "repent" of former sins and desire to lead a new life in anticipation of the coming Messianic age, in which such justice will find proleptic fulfillment for all in the kingdom of God.

In other words, these are not merely ethical mandates to be engaged but are, in fact, behavioral obligations that demonstrate both the desire to fulfill Old Testament mandates, and the proleptic realities of an emerging form of free obedience in the establishment of that form of divine justice to be evidenced in fullness in the coming kingdom of God, and therefore—like two mirrors facing off—reflect realities into the future that are also, always, and at the same moment, reflective and disclosive of past covenantal realities.

John the Baptist, as a central character in the narrative of the onset and development of a nascent form of gospel-infused graced freedom in the New Testament, does more than merely proclaim or preach, as preparation for the coming of the Messiah and the beginning of an age of a newly established graced freedom, he actually sets the wheels in motion for the eventuality of the gift of the gospel-based freedom, in and through Christ Jesus and the ministry of the gospel Christ incarnates and proclaims. John's ethical mandates are clearly associated with freedom for humanity, as each of them, in centrality of intent, directs actions to the establishment of justice and therefore the enrichment of justice-deprived human life; in free obedience to God and that which God has commanded, the faithful covenantal partner engages in behaviors that bring greater dignity to each person who has suffered—or could suffer—injustices associated with inhumanity and selfish disregard for the welfare of one's "neighbor." The establishment of genuine justice within the communal setting (whether local or global), when the precedent is that form of justice God requires, demands the presence and reality of freedom for humanity, where one's choices and actions cannot be divorced from the larger arena of concern for the "needs of the neighbor."

In John's reply to the specific ethical questions raised (see Luke 3:10–14) we overhear the reaffirmation of the command of God for the establishment and maintenance of a community of faith that would disclose to all the world the exact nature of the justice, mercy, compassion, and explicit care for the less fortunate—as well as the "sojourner"—which constitutes demonstration of free obedience to the will of God for the whole world. In exactly this way, all that John has stated as the necessary consequence of repentance and renewal is intended to demonstrate the establishment of the emerging messianic community of compassion as a foretaste of the future, climactic, and more cosmic kingdom of God. The mandates John establishes are, therefore, disclosive of a form of life in community that contributes, enormously, to preparations being put in place as anticipatory of the first advent of God's Messiah—the Messiah who now stands within John's audience waiting for the hour of disclosure. It is essential to a more inclusive understanding of the very nature of "sin" to lay hold of those manifestations of "sin" that show— in clear and concise ways—just how "sin" disrupts and damages both human nature as God intended it to be, and communal existence as the harmonious and supportive environment for the enrichment of humanity holistically (simply recall God's statement prior to the creation of Eve: "It is not good for man to be alone").

Both the questions raised and John's admonitions to follow indicate those ways in which "sin" corrupts and contaminates communal verities as well as the individual who has submitted to temptation and spiritual trial, and is therefore in bondage. For too many in the contemporary church "sin" is a matter of individual accountability, with little or no comprehension of the dire implications of "sin" for the violation and disruption of communal harmony, at both local and global levels! In anticipation of and in preparation for the coming of the Messiah, John reasserts that form of graced freedom evident throughout the old covenant and therefore also essential to the establishment of, what will come to be called, the "new covenant" and the "new covenant community."

A Pastoral Proposal for an Evangelical Theology of Freedom

What has been implicit thus far is now stated explicitly: there is no graced freedom that is evident outside the boundaries of the faith community—whether Israel or the Church—and John the Baptist, even though portrayed or characterized as one who stands outside the mainstream of the religious leadership of his own time, nevertheless stands within the traditions of the Old Covenant and the salvation-historical realities of Israel and her people. God's bestowal of graced freedom can only be nurtured in the soils of a faith community, simply because graced freedom is fundamental to faith and obedience in a covenantal context and intended to be a transformational reality in which both individual and community express their deepest sense of identity, before God and the world, as a people whose existence and fundamental purpose for living can be defined as "freedom for humanity." In the passage under consideration, John does not simply issue ethical or moral mandates; rather, John speaks from within the reality of graced freedom to assert those actions that disclose the promise of God's justice for Israel and the world beyond her borders as well. The standards John sets forth in his answer to those who seek guidance for their behavior are commendable because—like the Law itself—they are founded on grace; as grace these actions or behaviors are intended to enhance the freedom of faith that is the basis of covenantal obedience and trust in God, while disclosing to the world the advent of communal regard for human welfare as the keystone of God's coming kingdom (which will be proleptically realized even more dramatically and fully in the person and work of Christ Jesus).

This is not to suggest that there is no experience of "freedom" existing outside the boundaries of the covenantal communities of Israel and the Church; there are shadows or shades of "freedom" which always take form as "autonomy" (literally, "self-law" or "self-sufficiency") or perhaps "liberty" (as "freedom" from political coercion or tyranny) in the wider socio-political realm of existence (see the introduction to this essay); even in the realm of "religion" there can be manifestations of "freedom"—but graced freedom will only be discovered within the realm of the respective faith communities of Israel and the Church, as graced freedom can never be divorced from the aspect of covenantal verities essential to its nurture and development (read: "spiritual maturation"). Whereas these "shadows" of "shades" are actual manifestations of freedom, they touch upon externals more than they do bring about internal transformations of life; it is only graced freedom that involves the whole of one's life, restoring to the recipient that form and essence of humanity which was intended by God prior to

The New Testament Witness to Graced Freedom

"the fall of Adam and Eve." Graced freedom, as the gift of God, transforms the whole of one's life and living as is indicative of grace itself, and this by virtue of the fact that the presence of grace implies the presence of God in the power of the Holy Spirit, and the Spirit cannot be divorced from the living Lord Christ, as in the affirmation of the apostle Paul: "Now the Lord is the Spirit, and where the Spirit of the Lord is, there is freedom" (2 Cor. 3:17).

The necessary distinction to be made between the reality of graced freedom and those forms of freedom that, while real, fall short of bringing about the transformation of life essential to the extension of graced freedom as freedom for humanity, is taken up in more detail in the next chapter. For now we simply assert our contention: one of the primary distinctions between graced freedom and all other forms of freedom is that only graced freedom empowers the recipient to an externalization of *agapic* love, remaining focused on and committed to the pursuit and establishment of justice (as defined from within the limits of God's covenantal theology) for all people, and is therefore consistently and persistently a freedom for humanity, which is a proleptic manifestation of what will be realized in fullness in the coming kingdom of God.

Before we move on to consider the role of Mary as a model of graced freedom, there remain two significant passages from Luke's gospel that claim our attention; John the Baptist's biting words to the crowds who came for baptism (Luke 3:7–9) and John's affirmation of the distinction to be made between himself and his ministry and the Messiah (Luke 3:15–17). We turn first to Luke 3:7–9:

> [John] then said to the crowds who came out to be baptized by him, "Brood of vipers! Who warned you to flee from the coming wrath? Therefore produce fruit consistent with repentance. And don't start saying to yourselves, "We have Abraham as our father," for I tell you that God is able to raise up children for Abraham from these stones! Even now the ax is ready to strike the root of the trees! Therefore, every tree that doesn't produce good fruit will be cut down and thrown into the fire."

Implicit in the words of John is the distinction between "religion" and a sense of belonging associated with the privilege of being a member of the covenant, by virtue of a "religious rite" (i.e., circumcision), and "faith" as that internal transformation associated with graced freedom and the obedience that issues from the transformed, faith-infused heart of the believer.

The former is far more common, even in the time of the Baptist, as can be witnessed in the numerous encounters between Jesus and some of the religious leaders of his time, in which Jesus himself voices disapproval of reliance on ritual observations and covenantal membership as sufficient; the latter is the form of life God desires of those who would enter (freely and in faith) into the covenant established in grace, manifestly evident in the ministry of Jesus as the call to repentance and faith. The former is little more than a claim, with associated ritualistic practices (as seen in some of the Pharisees and Sadducees, in particular those of whom Christ was most critical) and places emphasis on a certain category of rigorous fulfillment of specific obligations (regardless of the condition of the heart); the latter comes from a heart that has been transformed so that all obedience discloses faith and freedom, regardless of any one ritual (with the exception of the "baptism for the forgiveness of sins"). The purpose for the bestowal of faith and the concomitant freedom is so that obedience and service to God will be given from a heart that has been radically converted to a new life, lived for humanity and for the humanization of a world that all too often dehumanizes.

The second passage to draw our attention is Luke 3:15–17:

> Now the people were waiting expectantly, and all of them were debating in their minds whether John might be the Messiah. John answered them all, "I baptize you with water, but One is coming who is more powerful than I. I am not worthy to untie the strap of His sandals. He will baptize you with the Holy Spirit and fire. His winnowing shovel is in His hand to clear His threshing floor and gather the wheat into His barn, but the chaff He will burn with a fire that never goes out.

This passage is not merely Luke's taking literary license with might have been the actual words of John, but serves a more theological purpose in distinguishing between the ministry of John as "forerunner" and that of the Messiah, whose ministry will be deeply transformational. John's importance is not diminished (even with John's statement: "He must increase, but I must decrease" [John 3:30]); but his role is further clarified in terms of the power to transform, implicit in his acknowledgment that while his baptism is with water, the baptism of the Messiah will be with the Holy Spirit and fire, a clear reference to the total transformation of one's life that comes from an open encounter with the Christ of God.

The New Testament Witness to Graced Freedom

As a manifestation of his own free obedience to the purpose for which God brought him into the world, John states what should be the posture of anyone who would confess Christ; he is no more than a servant who is not worthy to untie the strap of his sandals; this is not to be understood as self-deprecation, but rather a form of genuine humility that celebrates the gift of graced freedom through intentional and sustained submission to the Savior, and authentic obedience evidenced in enthusiastic service. The reference to the winnowing shovel and threshing floor serves to announce that, with the coming of the Messiah, there will also come a clarification of those ordained to either acceptance or rejection, which is based on acceptance or rejection of the Messiah, his person and message, an acceptance evident in one's submission to his baptism with the Holy Spirit and fire (in this instance, "fire" being a metaphorical image, associated with purification of a sacrifice made in obedience to the will of God).

Yet from this same passage one cannot overlook the reference to a coming judgment, obviously to take place with the first advent of the Messiah, which is also a proleptic event anticipating the "end time" judgment that will accompany the second advent or "return" of Christ in the future. The question becomes, what is the nature of graced freedom in relation to both the immediate and future judgments that transpire under the authority of the Messiah in both instances? John the Baptist does not delineate the exact nature of that judgment, other than by way of metaphorical imagery, that is, the separating of the "wheat" from the "chaff"—a classic form of imagery also associated in the teaching of Christ with the "end time" judgment. But the full measure of John's ministry and mission can only be understood as a proclamation of repentance and the reception of graced freedom in anticipation of Christ's judgment; the intent of John's baptism is as much anticipatory as is his purpose as the forerunner and one who is to prepare the way for the coming of the Messiah. Submission to the baptism John offers is but a prelude to the more comprehensive baptism with the Holy Spirit and fire that will initiate total transformation of the one submitting to the Lordship of Christ and the good news of salvation in his name; graced freedom assures the one who has undergone this messianic baptism that he or she will be counted among the "wheat" that is finally received into the fullness of God's coming kingdom. For the believer, who by virtue of graced freedom remains consistent in faith, Christ's judgment is both definitive purging and perfection of that which was initiated in and through faith, while for the non-believer the same event can only hold the dread of final separation from God.

What we are given in this characterization of John the Baptist is the example of graced freedom evident in a life that is lived—at its depth—in devotion to the will and way of God and in fulfillment of the purpose for which he was born into this world; John's faith, as the basis for the establishment of graced freedom in his life, must be assumed, as graced freedom can only be traced to the presence of faith in the covenant partner's life. The freedom exemplified in the life of John the Baptist is a freedom for humanity, in that the whole of John's focus is on the promised liberation from the bondage of sin and guilt as a consequence of submission to the baptism he performs in anticipation of the transformative baptism that will be realized in and through the ministry and message of Christ Jesus. In this way John demonstrates that any freedom for humanity must be holistic and concern itself with all aspects of human existence, and not merely with spiritual or socio-political realities; it must be a freedom willing to lay down its life for the enrichment and enlargement of human welfare under the guidance of the Holy Spirit and to the glory of God. What we witness in the person and ministry of John the Baptist becomes even more evident in Mary the mother of our Lord, the *theotokos*, to whom we now turn our attention.

MARY THE THEOTOKOS

> In the sixth month, the angel Gabriel was sent by God to a town in Galilee called Nazareth, to a virgin engaged to a man named Joseph, of the house of David. The virgin's name was Mary. And the angel came to her and said, "Rejoice, favored woman! The Lord is with you." But she was deeply troubled by this statement, wondering what kind of greeting this could be. (Luke 1:26–29)

The narrative of the Annunciation places Mary at the forefront of the singular event in the history of humankind, and places her there as a superlative example of faith and graced freedom, as she is called or chosen of God to bear the Christ-child—an honor of unparalleled significance and one demanding she be given her rightful place in the adoration of all Christians as *theotokos* and as the first to offer the whole of herself to the fullness of God's will, and in faith, as the vessel in the fulfillment of the Messianic promise to Israel and the world. We do not affirm this lightly, in full knowledge of the controversy that continues to swirl around any talk of "adoration" or

The New Testament Witness to Graced Freedom

"veneration" of Mary; but there can be no denying the centrality of her role—as clearly dramatized in at least two of the gospels (i.e., Luke and Matthew) and in the Book of the Acts of the Apostles as well—as a theological conviction demanding greater respect among Protestants of all confessional backgrounds! What we offer in this portion of the chapter is a reflection on Mary as a role model of graced freedom, the associated faith, submission to Christ as Lord, and obedience as the first among disciples. We will also contend that it is in this exact role that Mary exceeds all other efforts—and in particular those of the more radical feminists—to provide an exemplary model for what is often euphemistically referred to as "equality of the sexes" or justice for women in the church and in all areas of life.

To begin, where one might associate the significance or notoriety of Mary with the fact that she was betrothed ("engaged" is often misleading, as "betrothal" was much closer to marital obligations of fidelity, etc., than we would normally associate with being "engaged") to a man whose ancestry ran back to king David; in no small measure a religious and social distinction of paramount importance. But, while that fact serves to obliquely connect Christ to that same blood and ancestral line, the focus of this passage is on Mary (as we will see in more detail in all that follows) and the implications of her having been chosen of God for this high and most holy purpose, and on the incredible faith and courage she demonstrates in her act of submission to God's purpose and call, all of which commends her as a notable illustration of graced freedom.

The mere fact that Mary consented to become the earthly vessel for the embryonic Messiah demonstrates both faith and courage in that pregnancy in the period of betrothal would prove sufficient cause for her death. We must not overlook the words with which Mary is greeted by the angel Gabriel; in calling Mary the "favored one" Gabriel is not so much addressing her by some form of title, but is in fact acknowledging that she has the grace of God in abundance!

There is a sense in which this scene of the Annunciation replicates—or better said—foreshadows the more general call to discipleship, in that there is the word or gospel proclaimed with an embedded promise, the submission to the internalization of the Word in free obedience, and the numerous consequences (positive and negative) that follow as one bears the Christ within the womb of one's soul. In this sense Mary, as illustrative, is predecessor for all disciples who will enter into an intimate relation with the Christ of God; yet she surpasses all others in that her fiat in faith and free obedience brought the Messiah into the world for the salvation of all. The reference in our passage to Mary being "troubled" and wondering about the exact nature of the greeting is also representative of that form of humility of heart which is expected of all disciples; Mary is humbled by this greeting of a superlative nature, which elevates her as one who is "favored" in the sight of heaven and before the realm of God's holy angels. Gabriel's affirmation that the Lord "is with" Mary is indicative of the place she has been given in the heart of God as one chosen to play a most important role in the first advent of the Redeemer into the world. We confess that there is redundancy in what is being affirmed, but that is a necessary redundancy, as such a reflective focus on Mary as exemplary of faith, graced freedom, and obedience is unprecedented among most Protestant explorations of discipleship and therefore uncommonly unfamiliar to most in the Protestant confessions of Christian faith (an audience we assume to be our primary target). Nevertheless, we think it imperative that Mary find her rightful place in a theology of freedom for humanity.

The exchange between Mary and Gabriel, which follows immediately the passage we have just considered, is central to our exposition of Mary as exemplary of graced freedom and the obedience that flows from such divinely conferred freedom:

> Then the angel [Gabriel] told [Mary]:
> "Do not be afraid, Mary,
> for you have found favor with God.
> Now listen:
> You will conceive and give birth to a son,
> and you will call His name Jesus.
> He will be great
> and will be called the Son of the Most High,
> and the Lord God will give Him
> the throne of His father David.
> He will reign over the house of Jacob forever,
> and His kingdom will have no end."
> Mary asked the angel, "How can this be, since I have not been intimate with a man?"
> The angel replied to her:
> The Holy Spirit will come upon you,
> and the power of the Most High will overshadow you.
> Therefore the holy One to be born
> will be called the Son of God.

The New Testament Witness to Graced Freedom

> And consider your relative Elizabeth—even she has conceived a
>   son in her old age, and
> this is the sixth month for her who was called childless. For noth-
>   ing will be impossible
> with God."
> "I am the Lord's slave," said Mary, "May it be done to me according
>   to your word."
> Then the angel left her. (Luke 1:30–38)

Anyone with even a passing familiarity with biblical narrative is aware that "fear" or "being afraid" in the presence of any angelic visitation is common; there is only one reaction a human can have in the presence of such glory as would be displayed in any angelic visitation, and that is complete awe and consequent trembling! This is not the fear one would associate with a child's late night apprehensions about the dark; it is rather that form of astonishment that understandably accompanies any disclosure that is initiated by God or a "messenger" of God. Yet it is not so much the opening comforting word of Gabriel that catches our attention, as it is the reiteration of the statement that Mary has been "favored" by God—a superabundance of grace is here being acknowledged—a grace that exceeds even the most wild expectation of the human soul. Note, however, that this "favor" of God, which is pregnant with promise, is also and at the same time fraught with potential peril, which makes the response of Mary all the more compelling as a manifestation of the profound nature of the obedience associated with graced freedom.

Regarding the only question posed by Mary, it is curious that her query does not issue in the same result as that portrayed in the conversation between the angel and Zechariah, father of John the Baptist. A clue is perhaps found in the manner in which Zechariah frames his question, asking not, "How can this be?" but rather, "How can I know this?" Seemingly a question of skepticism, maybe even implicitly the request for a "sign" to validate the promising word of the angel. Mary poses a question that does not doubt the actuality of the word coming to fruition, but wonders aloud how such a thing is possible without the most commonly understood way in which pregnancy occurs, that is, by way of human intercourse. It is also a theological question, in that Mary is only too aware of Mosaic Law forbidding sexual relations prior to marriage; so the query could also be a plea to understand how this can be done without a violation of God's Law, which Mary (not unlike her betrothed partner, Joseph) would never consider an option—she, too, is a "righteous" person! We are simply pointing out the depth of Mary's character as one for whom obedience to the Law of the Lord is a fundamental expression of love and faith (recall that it is in Luke's account that Joseph and Mary attend to the Temple with the appropriate offering and to have their child circumcised, as proscribed by Mosaic Law and as a covenantal obligation).

Yet it is in Mary's fiat ("I am the Lord's slave . . . May it be done to me according to your word.") we are given the substantive expression of graced freedom manifest in complete submission to the will of the Lord God! Nothing would move beyond this brief encounter were it not for this generous expression of confessional and covenantal faith in the "word" of the Lord as presented by his own heavenly messenger, Gabriel. Mary does more than submit to the divine mandate set before her, she willingly and with genuine humility of heart places herself in the position of one whose entire purpose in life is to serve the will of the Lord God ("I am the Lord's slave"); there is nothing—even the risk of ridicule, ostracism, and death itself—that stands as an obstacle between Mary's love of God and her desire to devote herself to God's will for her, for humanity, and for the world. (Recall the words of first John: "There is no fear in love; instead, perfect love drives out fear, because fear involves punishment" [1 John 4:18].) Of course, fear of "punishment" was not at issue in the words of Mary, yet her fiat is a splendid expression of that perfection of love for God that overcomes all obstacles to obedience—as such love is also the fruit of graced freedom. Such love for God cannot be divorced from the other side of the two-fold commandment to love God and neighbor (Matt. 22:37–38); in this sense we affirm this expression of Mary's love of God as at the time an extraordinary expression of her love for her "neighbor"—or in the wider sense of that term—humanity in its concrete realities and not merely in the abstract.

Mary's fiat and her faithful submission to the will of God can only be rightly understood as an act of love for humanity in its plight, as a daughter of Israel and reared on the Scriptures of her people, Mary is aware of the human condition under sin and the wider effects of sin in the realm of socio-political realities. This broader understanding of sin and its adverse effects in the corporate realm of socio-political realities is evident in Mary's song of praise as recorded in Luke 1:46–55, in which Mary associates the gift of God's Promised One with the reversal of all circumstances of injustice—even to the degree that she has been elevated to a higher estate by virtue of God's having "favored" her as the one chosen to be the mother of the Lord Christ. The presence of graced freedom in her life is disclosed in Mary's expressed joy in what she perceives to be God's fulfillment of a

The New Testament Witness to Graced Freedom

promise made to her covenantal ancestors, and in her declaration that the coming of the Child she bears in her womb heralds an age of justice for those who have been deprived and the debasing of those who have lived unjustly, inflicting hardship on others, living in a manner contrary to the expressed will of God. The justice anticipated as one of the aspects of the messianic age is, of course, a proleptic event, as if much if not most of the glory associated with the first advent of the Christ. Even so, Mary's psalm of praise—in its confessional aspect—discloses the essential joy that arises in the heart and soul of one whose life has been flooded with and is compelled by graced freedom.

Luke's account of the birth of the Messiah (Luke 2:1–20) includes the visitation of the shepherds (Luke 2:8–20) in which we are given a glimpse of the reversals about to transpire in the coming kingdom of Christ, as a foreshadowing of the coming kingdom of God, where those at the lower end of the socio-political spectrum are the first to be honored with the message of the Messiah's birth and the first to behold him in his humble nursery. Those familiar with the narrative know that there is a one sentence description of Mary's reaction to the story of the angelic pronouncement regarding her child as told by the shepherds; Luke tells us that Mary was treasuring up these things in her heart and meditating on them (Luke 2:19). Here we are given another manifestation of the faith implicit in the heart and soul of this simple girl whose life has been blessed of God—and yet faces so much that will be painful (recall the words of Simeon to Mary following the circumcision of her child, "and a sword will pierce your own soul" (Luke 2:35a)! Only graced freedom can account for this mother's unquestioned obedience and commitment to the unfolding will and way of God for his Son, as manifest in the words of the shepherds and Simeon.

Finally, there is evidence of the obedience of Mary and Joseph to the will and way of God, disclosed in the presentation of the Christ child in the Temple and for the purposes of his consecration and entrance into the covenantal community through the ritual of circumcision. It is of vital importance that the Christ be circumcised and enter into the covenant of God with Abraham as an aspect of both his identity and ancestral lineage—as vital as will be his submission to the baptism of John—so that "all righteousness may be fulfilled"; together these ritual acts remove any question of Christ's "person and work" serving as the essential bond between the old and new covenants. Mary and Joseph demonstrate their commitment to the Abrahamic covenant by having their child circumcised, and in provision of the appropriate offering; throughout this narrative account Mary and

A Pastoral Proposal for an Evangelical Theology of Freedom

Joseph demonstrate the depth of free obedience that is the standard for all who love the Lord God with the fullness of heart, soul, mind, and strength; a love that is also and always demonstrated in care for the neighbor in need (see Luke 10:25–37) as a manifestation of graced freedom. God selected Mary and Joseph for this profoundly important role and it can be assumed that God made this choice on the basis of the faith and covenant character of these two members of Israel. Graced freedom is evident in the numerous ways in which both Mary and Joseph issue their "yes" to the expressed will of God, from the first troubling message of the angel to the bewildering encounter with their child in the Temple at the age of twelve and beyond. One of the most astounding pieces of evidence to the continued obedience of Mary and Joseph to the will of God for the life of this very special child is found in the closing verses of the second chapter of Luke's gospel: And (Jesus) went down (from Jerusalem) with (Mary and Joseph) and came to Nazareth and was obedient to them. His mother kept all these things in her heart. And Jesus increased in wisdom and stature, and in favor with God and with people (Luke 2:51–52).

In concluding this chapter we focus on two portions or passages already considered, and with the first, take some license, which is warranted by the text; we call attention to the final acclamation of Luke in the closing words of the passage sited at the conclusion of the last full paragraph: "And Jesus increased . . . in favor with God and with people." Every "good enough" parent would acknowledge that such an acclamation can, to a greater than lesser extent, be attributed to the guidance, nurturing, education, and care given the child by the parent(s). It only stands to reason that as two faithful Jews, Mary and Joseph would have attended with great care to the education of their child and to see that he was nurtured in the faith and traditions of their covenant community, and they would have seen to the development of their child's covenantal character with as much—if not more—devotion as that given to his physical welfare. In the film titled *The Nativity*, there is a marvelously imaginative scene in which Mary and Joseph ruminate on the future parenting of this incredible child she bears in her womb, and at one point Joseph wonders what, if anything, he will be able to teach this child, the assumption being that his knowledge would be far more limited than would be that of the Christ—even as a child. While this scene serves a dramatic effect, it is far more likely that Joseph and Mary, each in his or her respective role, played a vital part in the development of this child's life well into adulthood. We would dare to be bold in suggesting that they would have proven faithful to the tasks of parenting as a way of loving God and humanity, by doing—in all good faith—what would serve to enrich the covenantal character of this child. And for our purposes we also emphasize the striking claim that Jesus increased in favor with God and with people, noting that the term "favor" implies "grace" in the fullest sense of the singular characteristic that sets one apart as a person of faith and graced freedom; this is an exceptional affirmation of the parenting and faith of these two common, yet chosen, people in the singular form of obedience that proves exemplary for all who would seek to love God and neighbor as commanded.

Before advancing to our next chapter, we wish to address those readers of this essay who have found all of this focus on Mary as exemplary somewhat unorthodox (by traditional standards of Protestant exegesis and theology), that our intent has been to explore the characteristics of Mary's faith, as she is presented in the dramatic narrative of Luke's Gospel, and not simply as one of several historical personages to have played a key role in the first advent of the Christ. One must attempt to comprehend Mary as exemplary because of the central role she has as the Mother of our Lord and therefore, in the conciliar language of the church still honored among Orthodox Christians, as the *theotokos*. When we receive the testimony of St. Luke that, in response to Gabriel's message, Mary replied be it done to me according to your word (and here we take up exposition of our concluding passage) there is resonance of both graced freedom and the profound obedience that issues from such freedom. Moreover, this submission to the word of God's messenger can be said to resonate as well with that form of submission one expects to discover in the life of any one disciple of Christ, who is the Word of God incarnate!

A disciple of Christ cannot hope to follow in the faithful and obedient footsteps of the Mother of Christ in the absence of graced freedom; yet with the gift of graced freedom any follower is empowered to obey God's will and to follow in the way of the Savior, and in doing so to become a life that is lived as freedom for humanity in the pursuit of justice as defined by the commandments and covenantal obligations of God made evident in the life and death of our Savior. Since, as the apostle Paul has stated so eloquently, Christ is "in" us and we are "in" Christ, each Christian disciple is—in a minor sense of the term—a kind of "*theotokos*"—a bearer of Christ, our God, to the world and for the world. With this image in mind we turn to our next chapter and the marvelous theology of the apostle Paul.

4

The Testimony of Paul to Graced Freedom

"Christ has liberated us into freedom. Therefore stand firm and do not submit again to the yoke of slavery."

—GALATIANS 5:1

ALTHOUGH THE CORPUS OF the apostle Paul constitutes a rich and variegated texture of theological exposition and confessional affirmation, there can be no doubt that freedom is one of the central theological categories of Paul's thinking and proclamation. Granted, as evident in the passage quoted above, Paul's interest is often associated with the need to annunciate, in the clearest of terms, the present purpose (if any) of the law for the Christian (Paul is not antinomian, but is concerned with a particular understanding and usage of the law); it can and will be affirmed and demonstrated in this chapter that the theme of freedom, in a much broader context of understanding, is to be found throughout Paul's writings, even when it is more implicit than explicit in his theological explications. We are not returning to the once accepted practice of defining Paul's letters as if they were simply theological treatises of a kind; we merely wish to affirm that, even as a rabbinical student, Paul understood the centrality of theological insight and exposition as essential to the enrichment of the community of faith. The writings of the apostle Paul also bear testimony to the centrality of grace in his exposition of the gospel of Jesus Christ; both grace, and the freedom associated with grace, have become categorically essential to a fuller comprehension of the whole of the apostle's own proclamation of the Good News.

The HCB has it correct in translating the first sentence of Galatians 5:1 as "Christ has liberated us into freedom," because there is an important distinction to be made between the concept of having been liberated and the idea that such liberation has been into a unique form of freedom. Should one favor the translation of the RSV or other less dynamic translations of the same passage (i.e., "For freedom Christ has set us free"), the use of *set us free* itself implies a once and done act, where the concept of freedom as we have interpreted it remains in play. Additionally and by implication the freedom into which the Christian has been embedded—if you will—is not merely a conceptual understanding, but a form of life that will only find adequate expression in unqualified obedience to the will and way of God in Christ, as set forth in the whole of the gospel. To state the same in the simplest of terms: the freedom into which the Christian has been inserted is relational in character, grounded and sustained by a relationship with the living, reigning, Lord Christ in and through the power of the Spirit and consistently funded within the fellowship of the Body of Christ. Here we begin to see the initial glimmers of what will soon be the blinding light of Paul's explication of graced freedom, in that this same freedom, which is relational in character, is also fundamentally based on grace and grace alone; we will say more in this area latter in this chapter. Stressing the relational character of this freedom is absolutely imperative if we are to come to a full appreciation for the nature of graced freedom in the theology of the apostle Paul, as far more than a conceptual reality internalized (even if by faith) by the Christian and serving to sustain a sense of self-directed will.

The relational character of this freedom is comparable to the same relational character one should associate with the concept of covenant in both the Old and New Testaments; if covenant is comprehended as something less or other than relational in character, what is lost is the essential nature of the concept as disclosed in the history of salvation as recorded in both Old and New Testaments. We contend that the same can be affirmed of Paul's exposition of freedom (as relational), where grace (as a relational term) is essential in every way. Even though in Galatians the issue for Paul is liberation from the constraints of obedience bordering on what has traditionally, though imprecisely, been called works-righteousness (associated with the argument by some in the church of the necessity for Gentile Christians to be circumcised as the ritual act of entrance into the covenant of Abraham and associated obedience to the Mosaic law), Paul stresses a liberation into freedom implying a parallel entrance into the new covenant, which is only possible in and through a relationship—both personal and corporate—with/within Christ. On this point the thought of the apostle is not novel so much as it is a reframing of what was the original intent of the law, as grounded in grace and necessitating the covenant, where graced freedom assured that obedience itself would always be free obedience, as the most profound expression of the love of God associated with the covenantal relationship. In this context worship is more than liturgical engagement, whether on the Sabbath or, as with Christians, on the Lord's Day—the eighth day; worship is that lived expression of the love of God, evident in the open obedience each and every day and concurrent with genuine faithfulness in and to the new covenant relationship. As is proper to obedience in the realm of the covenant, the only true worship is free worship and the only free worship is funded by the (liberating) love of God and the desire for regular communion and fellowship with God in the Spirit of Christ (see Rom. 12:1).

The fact that the Christian has been liberated into freedom also means that this act of grace constitutes a liberation that is both from and for very particular realities, which though related are strikingly dissimilar in their outcome. The Christian has been liberated from (at least in the context of Galatians) any form of obedience that is, for all intents and purposes, little more than bondage to the internal drive to be accepted by God, for whom the consequences of sin bring both death and judgment. In having been graciously liberated from the consequences of both sin and judgment, the Christian has also and at the very same time been liberated from any internal drive to be accepted by God; that same acceptance comes in the person and work of Christ, and the embrace of Christ (by faith in the Christ—in both senses of the word in; i.e., that faith which is Christ's and that which comes to expression in the life of the Christian). The bestowal of graced freedom, as a direct consequence of his or her entering into a relationship with the living Lord Christ, and as the result of having been liberated from the former bondage, now makes possible that which could not be achieved before, and that is a freedom for obedience that is disclosive of love for God and externalized as love for humanity (love of one's neighbor).

If, as we have advocated throughout this essay, the willingness to sin cannot be comprehended as a free act, but can only be correctly understood as entering into a relationship of captivity and bondage to disobedience, than it only stands to reason that liberation from the power and consequence(s) of sin enables the one liberated to enter into graced freedom, enabling him or her to know the richness of God's love, forgiveness, mercy, and acceptance made actual in Christ and in a personal-communal relationship with Christ.

This graced freedom is not our possession, but is rather the freedom of Christ bestowed upon the Christian, who must stand firm within this relationship with the Redeemer if he or she is going to know the fruits of the freedom found only in Christ. The theological reality of the Christian existence as *simul justus et peccator* is not negated by the relationship he or she has in and with Christ; the theological phrase captures the reality of the Christian life as the enactment and expression of the freedom found in/with Christ, to obey and serve God and neighbor, as well as the presence of a sinful nature, which cannot be fully eradicated (contrary to those who claim perfection through piety in this life), but can be and is maintenanced through the presence of the Holy Spirit and by faith in Christ (both that faith which is Christ's conferred upon the believer, and that faith which is also an expression of graced freedom). If, as Paul would have it, sin is evident as slavery to all things contrary to the will of God in Christ, then freedom—as a spiritual reality—must be expressed in joyful obedience to Christ and the will of God for the believer's life to be lived in love, a love that resonates with that of Christ for humanity; in this sense, the freedom extended in Christ is freedom for humanity's enrichment. In such freedom the Christian discovers the capacity to do more than merely sympathize with the plight of his or her fellow human beings; he or she experiences a deep and profound empathy (i.e., a *pathos* with, as a form of vicarious participation in the suffering[s] of another); this essential *pathos* is what motivates the believer to care with Christ-like love and compassion for any one human being, just as Christ loved us and gave his life for the liberation of all humans enslaved in captivity to sin and its numerous destructions. And among those "destructions" would be those of a socio-political kind, demanding justice for those who are oppressed by unjust structures and systems, remembering, as we should, that the attainment of such justice is not the freedom we have been exploring, but resonates with such freedom at the level of socio-political liberation.

However, it is clearly evident from his epistles that the concern of the apostle Paul—or perhaps one should say, Paul's primary concern—is not with what can be attained by the disciple of Christ in the socio-political realm, but the far more urgent and critical need of humanity for freedom from the bondage of sin, disobedience to the Lord, and the denial if not rejection of all things holy that sin dictates. We will see that, for Paul, the following is the case: because sin is contrary to the intention and will of God for both creature and creation, bondage to sin is also contrary to God's desire for both and can only be remedied by redemptive freedom from sin and for relational obedience to and love for God and one's neighbor in need. And even if one should desire to restrict Paul to a debate regarding the Christian and the demands of the Mosaic Law, it can be asserted without equivocation that the apostle to the Gentiles has a very real concern to preserve the freedom (attributable to God and grace alone) of the believer from any form of bondage to the restrictions those in opposition to Paul's teaching and mission wished to place on Gentile converts to the faith.

Turning once again to Galatians, Paul writes to his brothers and sisters in Christ, saying: "For you were called to be free, brothers; only don't use this freedom as an opportunity for the flesh, but serve one another through love" (Gal. 5:13). This profound theological movement from "freedom" to "love" (i.e., the love of Christ evident in the life of the individual believer and the corporate body) affirms the central purpose for that freedom God has actualized in Christ, and asserts the necessary connection between that same freedom (as an ontological reality) and consequent expression of love (*agapē* as both consequential gift and ethical imperative). The indicative of the freedom actualized by virtue of God's redemptive event, in Christ and through the presence and power of the Holy Spirit, is coupled with the imperative of the "love command" of Christ Jesus (see John 13:34; Gal. 5:14), forming one seamless assertion. The freedom conferred by God in Christ is not to be misused for advancing the purposes of any one selfish or self-promotional intention (which would be to lay hold of an opportunity for the flesh), that is, to seek the enlargement of one's own life at the expense of others; rather this freedom finds its most profound outlet in loving service to the "neighbor" in the broadest sense of the term (as brother or sister in Christ, of course, but also as sojourner in the midst of the faith community, and as the neighbor in need in concrete realities).

Arguably one of the most profound affirmations of this freedom is located in Paul's second letter to the Corinthians, where he writes: "Now the Lord is the Spirit, and where the Spirit of the Lord is, there is freedom" (2 Cor. 3:16); an assertion that ministry and mission are dependent on the presence and power of the Lord Christ, and therefore dependent on the empowerment of the Spirit. This affirmation bears decisively on the entire issue of both the origin and intended purpose for such freedom as obedience that is manifest as love (again, love of God and neighbor in Christ) and not merely rote attendance to the demands of the law; there is a more glorious form of obedience that has been both disclosed in Christ and subsequently conferred upon Christ's followers (as grace) through the intercession of the Spirit. Only this form of freedom makes possible (and real) that obedience God has desired from the people of covenant from the beginning; as coercion is not conducive to obedience in any meaningful sense of the term, it is only in and with such graced freedom that genuine obedience takes on those characteristics reflective of the Spirit's presence and therefore a replication of the obedience of Christ Jesus. And one must not limit the presence of the Spirit to either the individual or the corporate body of believers, as this graced freedom is essential (the life-blood, if you will) of both the individual and the gathered body of believers. This is one of the characteristics that sets the Church catholic apart from all other institutional and organizational realities; the Church (and each contributing/participating member of her life) is ontologically grounded in a freedom that is uniquely a characteristic of Christ Jesus, and therefore uniquely a characteristic of the Church catholic as his body. Obviously the apostle Paul affirms the theological exclusivity of the church (as the body of Christ) among other institutions, but only because he asserts this graced freedom as the hallmark of such "exclusivity," which is, ironically, the very same hallmark singular to the church as a community of freedom created to serve Christ in serving God and humanity.

Generally speaking, if there is one aspect of the contemporary church that can be said to disclose a sense of self-identity contrary to that affirmed by the apostle, we would contend it is here, in this essential comprehension of graced freedom, which serves as the foundation of all that she is and all that she does. There can be little doubt that, in most of her confessional and denominational forms, the church is struggling to express, in clear and unambiguous terms, exactly what she is and how what she is stands at the heart and soul of her genuine exclusivity in relation to all other forms of religious belief and/or institutional construct. In a climate in which the church is treated with contempt, placed in the pot-luck of relativistic religious convictions, or what is far worse, simply ignored as irrelevant to contemporary realities, there is a sense of urgency in the effort to discover "what will work," or how it is that the Christian faith can speak meaningfully to those who have become "secularized." We will discuss this issue in our closing chapter, but for now will assert our pastoral conviction that when the Church catholic reclaims the transcendently-conferred identity (in Pauline terms: where the Spirit of the Lord is, there is freedom) as a body governed by the Spirit of Christ, who has gifted her with that form of freedom—disclosed in his incarnation, life, death, resurrection, ascension, and current reign at the right hand of the Father—which is uniquely her gift from God, will she cease to struggle with the issue(s) of identity, and recognize her essential task as proclamation of the gospel in service to God and humanity, which is the concrete manifestation of that same graced freedom in genuine obedience.

We also contend that it is in the sacraments of Baptism and Eucharist[1] that such graced freedom is celebrated in and by the community of faith, and yes, for the world as well; both Baptism and Eucharist are worshipful and ritualistic representations of the extent to which graced freedom is always freedom for humanity! As both sacraments cannot be properly understood without recognition of the centrality of Christ and the Trinitarian dynamic of each of the two sacraments, we contend that with Baptism graced freedom in conveyed (even if only in nascent form as "seed faith freedom") and within the celebration of the Eucharist graced freedom nurtures and sustains faith in the process of maturation (our being conformed to the "image of Christ"). Baptism and Eucharist serve as the liturgical environments in and through which the Spirit moves to initiate (in Baptism) the gift of graced freedom and nourishes (in the Eucharist) the gift of faith and the presence of graced freedom; in both sacramental encounters, the recipient is blessed with a freedom unparalleled—the freedom to be and

---

1. While acknowledging that the number of sacraments differs from one confessional tradition to another and from East to West, we nevertheless restrict ourselves to the two sacraments embraced by most Protestant traditions and recognized by those confessional communities engaged in ecumenical dialogue(s). This is not to imply that those remaining sacraments celebrated by other confessional communities are exceptions to what is being affirmed in terms of graced freedom; it is rather that we lack sufficient expertise in the explication of the remaining sacramental realities to state intelligently the applicability of graced freedom to their essential nature as sacraments of the Church.

The Testimony of Paul to Graced Freedom

become in fullness all that the Lord God desires him or her to be and become in Christ.

In his discussion of the "new life" to be discovered in Christ, Paul writes this to the Romans: "How can we who died to sin still live in it? Or are you unaware that all of us who were baptized into Christ were baptized into His death? Therefore we were buried with Him by baptism into death, in order that, just as Christ was raised from the dead by the glory of the Father so we too may walk in a new way of life" (Rom. 6:3–4). One could reasonably argue that Paul is here primarily concerned with the necessity of making it quite clear that one who has been baptized cannot live in sin (as a way of life unrepentant); but it is also evident, in stressing the reality of one's having "died" and been "buried" with Christ in/through baptism, that Paul intends to emphasize the reality of the "new life" as a life of faithfulness and obedience (which would obviously include the capacity to confess one's sin[s] and repent). The reality of this transformation of the one baptized can only be understood as a sacramental certainty in which the Spirit actualizes in the life of the one baptized the gracious gift of new life revealed in the crucified and risen Lord Christ; this new life includes the conference of graced freedom as the spiritual empowerment for obedience to God as an act of love. This is, at least in part, the significance of Paul's confessional affirmation in Galatians (2:19b–20): "I have been crucified with Christ and I no longer live, but Christ lives in me. The life I now live in the body, I live by faith in the Son of God, who loved me and gave Himself for me." While we do not wish to detract from the importance of the apostle's concern in this epistle, that is, Paul's focus on the relationship between the Mosaic law and the new life to be found in Christ and received in/by faith, it is also evident that Paul wants to convey the radical nature of the graced freedom that has been given in the Spirit of Christ, and the manner in which such freedom makes real a form of obedience that was not possible prior to the advent of Christ and the gracious bestowal of the Holy Spirit, a freedom and consequent obedience now evident in the life of the Christian and the Church. To be "in Christ" and have the Spirit of Christ "in you" means, essentially, to have become a person who has been and continues to be transformed, conformed to the image of Christ and impressed with those characteristics of Christ that exemplify graced freedom as faithful obedience to the will and way of God, that is, walking in a new way of life (Rom. 6:4).

Turning attention now to the Eucharist as what we would call the liturgical celebration of the joyous freedom found in communion with Christ at present and as anticipation of the fulfillment of that same graced freedom in the coming kingdom of God, we admit from the outset that there is no one passage of the Pauline corpus that overtly associates the Eucharist with freedom. Nevertheless, there is implicit in the apostle's theological explication of the relationship between the Eucharist and the Church herself hints of graced freedom sufficient to support our contention that this sacrament nurtures and sustains the freedom of the Christian, making his or her commitment to Christ and obedience to the Lord stronger. Our explication begins on a negative note with Paul's admonition to the Corinthians: "I hear that when you come together as a church, there are divisions among you" (1 Cor. 11:18); Paul will elaborate the basis of his contention with a discussion of the distortion in practice that the Corinthians have made in their celebration of the Eucharist: "when you come together, it is not really to eat the Lord's Supper" (1 Cor. 11:21). Notice the relationship implied in coming together as a church and coming together to eat the Lord's Supper, which would suggest that, with Paul, there is a direct correlation between what it means to be church in the context of worship and the proper celebration of the Lord's Supper as paramount to the essential nature of the church at worship.

If, as the apostle contends in Galatians (see Gal. 3:28) the church is one in Christ Jesus, then clearly it is an affront to Christ's body to practice the Lord's Supper as a meal intended to buttress distinctions that only divide, thereby disclosing a lack of appreciation for the graced freedom that has dismantled all such distinctions, broken down those barriers that once created social divisions; graced freedom can only be properly disclosed in a celebration of the Eucharist that affirms the oneness of this body of believers. In the Eucharistic celebration the one bread and one cup symbolize the one body of Christ, the unity of the Church, and the unity of the graced freedom that has given birth to this unparalleled community of faith. In this sense alone can the Eucharist become a liturgical celebration of the new humanity made possible in Christ, as the Church; in the image of her Lord and in the obedience of graced freedom conferred by the Spirit, the Church is broken and poured out in love for humanity and the world. Thus what looks, on the surface, like merely another religious ritual (i.e., the Eucharist) is, in fact and at its deepest level, a Spirit infused liturgical proclamation and assertion of the gospel truth that in Christ, and through the reality of graced freedom, God has created a "new covenant" community whose essential nature is to be a people devoted to the enrichment of human life in Christ.

Both Baptism and the Eucharist disclose the essential nature of the Church catholic as a community of faith, established and sustained by the presence of the Holy Spirit, with graced freedom as the basis of her mission and ministry in obedient love of God and faithful service to the whole of humanity in those ways that serve to enrich human life. Sacramental realities are also the ritual or liturgical affirmations of the authenticity of graced freedom; as practices infused with the grace of God in the power of the Holy Spirit, sacramental realities signify the worshipful disclosure of graced freedom as freedom given by the Lord God and for humanity—that is to say—for the manifest enrichment of humanity at every level of existence. Sacramental realities also disclose to the world the joyful obedience of the people of God, whose obedient spirit flows from a freedom unparalleled, because it encompasses the whole of the individual—heart, mind, body, soul, and spirit, while serving as the foundational reality of the community of faith. The heart that beats in the breast of the "Body of Christ" is strong in freedom because it is a heart that flows with the enriched spiritual blood of the Holy Spirit's power; this same heart is filled with compassion for the wounds of humanity and the numerous ways in which the Satan has bound humanity in sin and dis-grace. As both Baptism and the Eucharist embody the truth of new life to be found in Christ, and the consequent graced freedom with which the believer is empowered to commit his or her life to God, they also dissolve the chains by which Satan holds the human heart, soul, and spirit captive to the sin and its dreadful consequences.

Finally, and in conclusion to this chapter, we consider the affirmation of the words found in Colossians (3:11) in which it is declared that, "In Christ there is not Greek and Jew, circumcision and uncircumcision, barbarian, Scythian, slave and free; but Christ is all and in all." The reality indicated is relevant first and foremost—if not solely—to the community of faith as the body of Christ in which Christ determines both the identity and the commonality of character for the individual members of this new community and therefore of the entire community collectively. This is an identity and character transcending all previous forms of self-identification, whether religious, cultural, social, or ethnic in nature. Each and all together are now identified with the reality of Christ Jesus, whose presence establishes and sustains this unique identity—as we have stated above—in and through the sacramental realities of the church as the body of which Christ alone is the head. The dismantling of previous identity markers is another consequence of the provision of graced freedom in that one no longer is bound to those traits that were defined by the associated grouping, whether ethnic, religious, social, or cultural in nature. In and with such freedom comes the obedience that is manifest in love and unity of being and purpose, as indicated in the author's own words: "Therefore, God's chosen ones, holy and loved, put on heartfelt compassion, kindness, humility, gentleness, and patience, accepting one another and forgiving one another if anyone has a complaint against another. Just as the Lord has forgiven you, so you must also forgive. Above all, put on love—the perfect bond of unity. And let the peace of the Messiah, to which you were also called in one body, control your hearts" (Col. 3:12–15). The manifest expressions of the identity and character, established by virtue of Christ's gift of graced freedom and the consequent obedience as love, are associated with the very same characteristics of identity one would attribute to Christ himself! Such is also the deepest motivation for the externalization of this love out and into the world, where there are still those who have not realized the full measure of their humanity—disclosed in Christ and as God created humanity to be—due to their slavery to sin and the Satan's charge.

Note should also be given to the way in which the categories of unity, love, the peace of the Messiah, and the call to be in one body are in some sense related to the human heart, which among other characteristics is associated with the volition. This new life in Christ—this life of obedience by way of graced freedom—while perhaps centered in the heart—is not restricted to the heart, but as we have already stated, engulfs the whole of human life. Nevertheless, it is critical to recognize that the peace spoken of in the passage quoted above has its parallel in the Old Testament concept of *shalom* which is the peace of God's reign, to be found principally in the kingdom of God and as that harmony of creature and creation made possible because of the presence of the Holy Spirit; in this sense the peace of the Messiah—as the present *shalom* of the body of Christ, which anticipates a future fulfillment in the coming kingdom of God—is corporate in nature and is a powerful appearance of graced freedom as freedom for humanity within the existence of, what is often referred to in the Reformed tradition as, the "Church Militant."

The "battle"—if you will—is being fought for the very "soul" of humanity, or as has been said, to make and to keep human life human; graced freedom has been given not solely for the enrichment of the individual soul, but as a crucial component in the formation of a community of faith in which individuals have been freed to obediently serve God in loving service to the neighbor in need. The Church catholic lives as a spiritually-combative community that recognizes the Satan's tactic of debasing humanity by corrupting the soul and contaminating the spirit, heart, and mind of each and every person created *imago Dei*; such combat would not be possible where those committed to the conquering Christ not free from the entanglements of sin and its terrible consequences and through such graced freedom able to serve Christ in and through obedient love.

It would be no stretch of the imagination to tag the apostle Paul the "apostle of graced freedom" as such underlines the whole of his own writings and the entire Pauline corpus as well; that is not to overstate the case, as we have demonstrated in this chapter the centrality of the concept of freedom to the theology of Paul and to his proclamation of Christ's gospel. Of course the list of passages spread throughout the epistles of Paul could have been extended well beyond those cited, but that would require a book far more expansive than this, and would entail a much greater attentiveness to the exegetical commentary available.

We do believe that the case has been made for the importance—or more accurately stated, centrality—of what we are calling "graced freedom" to Paul's thought, and hope to follow this work with a much larger work exploring in greater exegetical detail the same theme in the wider field of the entire Pauline corpus of writings. Our only regret is that the space of the present essay is not conducive to a far greater elaboration of the importance of liturgy and sacramental realities in Paul's explication and affirmation of graced freedom as essential to the Church's witness to the world, and the externalization of such graced freedom in both her ministry and mission as a freedom for humanity in every meaningful sense of the phrase.

Freedom for humanity is evident in the revelation of God in Christ, and by the gift of graced freedom evident in and through the body of Christ—the church—which, under the empowerment of the Spirit, now lives out an obedient love in seeking to advance the claim of Christ on the whole of humankind through her proclamation of the gospel in word and deed, celebrated in the context of worship each and every Lord's Day, and manifest in (at least) the sacramental realities of both Baptism and Eucharist. Those characteristics annunciated in Colossians, that is, compassion, kindness, humility, gentleness, and patience, are beyond doubt mandated for expression within the body, but are also intended for externalization so that the "world" will witness humanity as God created it to be—in all its richness and fullness—and subsequently see more clearly the bondage to a lesser form of humanity that the Satan seeks to promote through slavery to his will and way.

A Pastoral Proposal for an Evangelical Theology of Freedom

We draw this chapter of our essay to a close with reference made to Romans 8:20–21, and in particular, the latter part of verse 21, which reads: "the creation itself will also be set free from its bondage of corruption into the glorious freedom of God's children." The passage resonates with eschatological anticipation that has now a proleptic reality, whose fulfillment is suspended in promise; nevertheless, not unlike the narrative of Christ's transfiguration (Matt. 17:2; Mark 9:2) the promise of a consummated freedom is a certainty already disclosed in the person and work of Jesus Christ. In this way the passage extends the promise of graced freedom well beyond the confines of humanity to include the entire creation—the cosmic order of the "world." This eschatological dimension to graced freedom is central to the gospel message of salvation and to all hope for the future fulfillment of that which has been revealed in and accomplished by Christ.

The passage quoted above also discloses the reality of God's having suspended, as an act of love, direct or forceful intervention into the horrific circumstance brought on by sin, as such would be an affront—if not a violation—of God's own desire to honor the free volition of both creature and creation. If, as Christ maintained, some had attempted to force their way into the kingdom of God (see Matt. 11:12; Luke 16:16), than clearly forcing his will on creature and creation is not the venue God would choose. Yet, in loving regard for the freedom of volition, which is as much an aspect of prelapsarian creation/creature as any other, God chose to send his Son into the world for the purposes of redemption and the re-introduction of graced freedom as one of the essential benefits of Christ to creature and creation. The consummation of that same freedom is suspended in the promise that is Christ, and this final freedom will also be the basis of an eternal and worshipful obedience on the part of both creature and creation, disclosing their essential nature as reflective of the honorary title—God's children.

The externalization of the same (and other) characteristics will awaken, within those presently bound by the Satan, the desire to embrace the graced freedom available in and through Christ alone, willingly becoming servants of the Lord who has promised his servants a fullness of life—and therefore an enrichment and enlargement of their humanity—unequaled! The centrality of the liturgical (i.e., worshipful) expression and affirmation of graced freedom as a freedom for humanity is, perhaps, no more dramatically exemplified than in the Book of Revelation, to which we turn our attention in the next chapter.

5

The Book of Revelation: Freedom for Humanity

"Then I saw a new heaven and a new earth, for the first heaven and the first earth had passed away, and the sea no longer existed. I also saw the Holy City, the new Jerusalem, coming down out of heaven from God, prepared like a bride adorned for her husband. Then I heard a loud voice from the throne: Look! God's dwelling is with humanity, and He will live with them. They will be His people, and God Himself will be with them and be their God. He will wipe away every tear from their eyes. Death will no longer exist; grief, crying, and pain will exist no longer, because the previous things have passed away."

—REVELATION 21:1–4

THE BOOK OF REVELATION has, regrettably, often been the object of some of the most extreme interpretations and bizarre applications, with most though not all having to do with some notion of "end time" speculation. That will not be the focus of our attention, as we consider this text to be, in actuality, more like an epistle than it is a "book." Two points of clarification need to be established from the outset: First, we do not interpret this document simply in terms of the so-called "end of days," recognizing, as we do, that eschatological imagery has as much to do with the past and present as it does the future. Second, we read this text against the background of a church under the fires of persecution, hounded to death by a brutal socio-political empire—that is, Rome, suggesting that this prophetic vision is intended for the entire world, as well as the community of faith under fire. In other words, to some degree, though not the only reason, the often startling imagery of Revelation is a decisive and intentional way of addressing, in literary form, issues of injustice and disharmony related to the whole of humanity, and not merely the immediacy of the churches being persecuted. It is a dramatic (and liturgically positioned) affirmation of the Lordship of God in Christ over all forces of oppression and draconian political machinations. Yet the often bizarre imagery discloses such injustices as having their origin in Satan's attempt to establish his own lordship over the earth and his desire to destroy the church of Christ. What is perceived as purely a matter of political injustice and persecution is revealed—at a far deeper level—to be a manifestation of Satan's efforts to thwart the fulfillment of God's plan of salvation for the entire world, and his twisted desire to establish his own reign over all the earth.

While the term "freedom" is not used in this epistle, it is our contention that graced freedom (as we have defined the term) is implicit throughout Revelation as the basis of the church's very existence in Christ and as the context of what will one Day be fulfilled in the coming kingdom of God. More importantly, we assert that both the environment and the focus of this epistle is not so much the unfolding or unveiling of any singular "end-time" scenario, so much as it is a prophetically-dramatic depiction of the way in which God has chosen to disclose his ultimate will for both the church and the world. This epistle is also the church's way of disclosing the centrality of graced freedom to the entire process of liberation for both creature and creation, while at the same time affirming that worship represents the setting in which the proclamation of Christ as Lord of all is most intensely dramatized and anticipated. That which has already been accomplished in Christ (the past) cannot be undone, and the impact of salvation in Christ (the present) is evident in the reality of graced freedom as the strength of the church's ministry and mission to humanity, while the historical fact of all that has been set in motion in God's gracious gift of the Messiah presses on to necessary fulfillment (the future) and serves as the internal strength, enabling the church to endure any and every form of hardship.

Of course, one need not be restricted to Revelation in asserting the importance of apocalyptic imagery to the whole of the gospel and New Testament witness to Christ, as there are numerous passages in which apocalyptic pictures serve as the background for proclamation of God's definitive victory over all the forces of bondage and oppression, which are the trademark of Satan's warfare against the good God intends for both creature and creation, for the entire cosmos. And such imagery has its origin in canonical Old Testament passages, as well as extant writings. These roots in the Old Testament corpus also demonstrate the prophetic edge to any and all apocalyptic expressions, not in the sense of prediction (although some of that genre is clearly implied in certain apocalyptic communications), but more importantly in the sense that these uncommon images bear the weight of proclaiming the will and way of God are gracious judgment on sin and the promise of final deliverance from the forces that hold both the people of God and humanity in bondage and captivity. What is said in the first chapters of Revelation would suggest that the churches being addressed (although in some manner faithful to God), have fallen short of serving God in that form of obedience graced freedom makes possible. In short, they have fallen back into the sinful practices that are indicative of a former bondage from which they had been liberated (read: saved) in Christ. This prophetic word to the seven churches of Asia is intended then to call them back, through repentance, to a more faithful posture in relation to their Lord, in anticipation of the coming victory of God in Christ over all forces of Satan, and in the full assurance that God's absolute reign will be established in the future.

However, the central theme of Revelation appears to be the final conquest of God over all evil and forces of evil that currently war against the work of the church and her people, while at the same time holding humanity in the vice-grip of dehumanization, destruction, and the dismantling of every form freedom takes in human existence and in the created order. The intent of evil appears to be more than what is normally associated with sin (i.e., as moral misconduct or relational disruption), as Satan intends the complete annihilation of all that is good in God's *ekklēsia* and creation, placing the whole of humankind, together with the whole of the cosmic order, in bondage (see Rom. 8:21) to a servitude that mimics obedience that is due solely to the Lord and his Christ. We say "mimics" because the obedience Satan demands of his subjects is anything but freely given; it is enforced slavery to the "lord" whose desire is complete destruction of all that God holds dear. The enslaved subject of Satan lives with a diminished sense of the value of the human soul before God, when the "soul" is properly understood as the essential self of each and every person, that is, the divinely bestowed essence of "who" he or she is as a child of God. In

A Pastoral Proposal for an Evangelical Theology of Freedom

this way submission to temptation is understood to be compliance with the desires of Satan and subsequent bondage to his beckon call; repentance (see Rev. 3:19), as the vehicle of liberation from such bondage, is always preceded by an act of genuine confession, and subsequently followed by the restoration of faith by virtue of the free gift of forgiveness; both faith and forgiveness come to restore graced freedom to the soul, conferred once again in the power of the Holy Spirit.

In order to properly understand our interpretation of this cryptic book, one needs to see that the Satan is the source of each and every form of bondage, which is why his presence is so ubiquitous throughout Revelation, and in a variety of grotesque imagery, even in those forces external to the Church that are persecuting her and hounding her to death, that is, the churches being addressed by John the prophet. Whether John is prophetically addressing the believers within the Church who have fallen away from the faith, or are at risk of doing so by way of disillusionment due to the deferred return of Christ, or attempting to dramatize the eventual and harsh judgment of a wrathful God on those responsible for her hardship and persecution—as the restoration of justice, the essential struggle (we contend) is dramatized as taking place between the reality of bondage in many forms and the establishment of graced freedom as the force for reconciliation and renewal. And worship (the liturgical stage) plays a central role in this dramatization because it is in the context of the liturgy, the people of God gathered for word and sacrament, that the message of graced freedom was re-asserted and received (with "gladness and simplicity of heart" [Acts 2:46]) as a beleaguered Church breathed in the fresh winds of the Holy Spirit.

This is not an attempt to provide a full-blown or extensive exegesis of Revelation, neither will we attempt to interpret the apocalyptic imagery that forms such an important part of this entire text; instead, as in previous chapters, we will be selective in choosing those passages held to be paradigmatic of our theme.

> After this I looked, and there in heaven was an opened door. The voice that I had heard speaking to me like a trumpet said, "Come up here, and I will show you what must take place after this. Immediately I was in the Spirit, and a throne was set up in heaven . . . Four living creatures covered with eyes in front and in back were in the middle and around the throne. The first living creature was like a lion; the second living creature was like a calf; the third living creature had a face like a man; and the fourth living creature

was like a flying eagle . . . Whenever the living creatures give glory, honor, and praise to the One seated on the throne, the One who lives forever and ever, the twenty-four elders fall down before the One seated on the throne, worship the One who lives forever and ever, cast their crowns before the throne, and say:

Our Lord and God,
You are worthy to receive
glory and honor and power,
because You have created all things,
and because of Your will
they exist and were created. (Rev. 4:1–2a; 6b–7; 9–11)

The drama unfolds in the context of the heavenly throne room and is laced with imagery common to the liturgy of the Church, including what is apparently an illusion to the four gospels (traditionally symbolized as "lion, calf, man and eagle") as creatures with "eyes" that, respectively, look both to the past and to the future.[1] What is fascinating is the manner in which John's vision takes place within the context of an environment that would have been familiar to most of his hearers-readers, that is, a worshipful setting; which places the drama itself within this same context as the most appropriate context in which it can be shared and comprehended. It is also evident that the reference to the "throne" and to the One seated upon the same, while situated in a worship setting, is a symbolic representation of the gauntlet being laid down against all those earthly powers (i.e., "thrones") that have abused both their office and power in demanding more than the rightful loyalty and obedience of their citizenry, having commanded that they be worshipped as divine and obeyed without question of their authority. The injustices perpetrated against the people of God as but one consequence of this abuse of office; the greater offense to the true Lord being the presumption of divinity and usurpation of the worship, reverence, and obedience that is rightfully his and his alone!

It is also captivating to see the manner in which this contrasting assertion of the Lord's rightful place as Sovereign over all other "thrones" is made within the context of a worshipful location, which would suggest that

---

1. We are aware that some interpreters find in these images a symbol for the whole of creation as represented by each of the four beings; however, while not denying that this may have been the author's intent, we also believe that, as is true with the symbolism of John's Revelation, these images are often open to more than one representation, and in this case (i.e., the context of worship in heaven) to reference to the symbolism of the four Gospels also seems to us a viable possibility for another interpretation.

for the Christian experiencing the traumas of injustice and persecution, worship on the Lord's Day would be essential to strengthening his or her resolve in remaining faithful and obedient to the One who is truly "Lord of all," as Creator and Redeemer of humankind, as the One *kurios*. Therefore, it is not an exaggeration of exegetical art to suggest that, in this perspective, liturgy, or the worship of the people of God, becomes a "political" assertion as well. In this way the one in worship is reassured that the extremities of suffering under persecution are not foreign to the Lord; his gospel "sees" the situation of sin and its socio-political consequences clearly! And the Lord's Sovereignty has not been conceded to those who rule with injustice and illegitimately lay claim to complete devotion, because Christ has already conquered all powers of the devil, death and destruction. Even though, as John's vision makes clear, this conquest of Christ has not yet been completed (it is proleptic), at least in part this prophetic letter reasserts the promise of a coming consummation.

We have already stated that one should not look to Revelation to provide any form of systematic/doctrinal beliefs, and in particular our theme of graced freedom; nevertheless one can surmise, from this first setting of the vision, that worship is commonly the context in which such freedom is reaffirmed as essential to faith and the continuation of hope in Christ as Lord, even under the most trying of circumstances. This is a freedom that transcends that which either capitulation to claims of the Caesar will provide the believer facing immanent persecution, or any other form freedom takes in the socio-political realm of order; as transcendent, this graced freedom empowers the recipient to remain committed to the Christ of freedom and to the ministry of liberation for those who are being victimized by an unjust and even brutal political machine. Whenever the Christian, in worship on the Lord's Day, vocalizes his or her confession of Christ as the One "worthy" to receive "glory and honor and power," the opening scene from John's Revelation assures him or her that such praise and confessional affirmation is resonant with the same claim be articulated in "heaven" and by those who have already conquered in Christ (i.e., the "twenty-four"). This is the liturgical assertion of graced freedom's power to prevail in the life of the believer and declares his or her obedience to him who is rightfully his or her Lord, as Lord of the Church catholic and as Lord of the whole of the created order.

The scene placed between the opening of the sixth and seventh seals is, once again, a worshipful event serving as an intermezzo to the climatic opening of seventh seal; because of this segments significance to our proposal, we have chosen to provide it in detail:

The Book of Revelation: Freedom for Humanity

"After this I looked, and there was a vast multitude from every nation, tribe, people, and language, which no one could number, standing before the throne and before the Lamb." They were robed in white with palm branches in their hands. And they cried out in a loud voice:
Salvation belongs to our God,
who is seated in the throne,
and to the Lamb!
All the angels stood around the throne, the elders, and the four living creatures,
And they fell facedown before the throne and worshiped God, saying:
Amen! Blessing and glory and wisdom
and thanksgiving and honor
and power and strength
be to our God forever and ever. Amen.
Then one of the elders asked me, "Who are these people robed in white, and where did
they come from?
I said to him, "Sir, you know."
Then he told me:
"These are the ones coming out of the great tribulation.
They washed their robes and made them white
In the blood of the Lamb.
For this reason they are before the throne of God,
And they serve Him day and night in His sanctuary.
The one seated on the throne will shelter them;
They will no longer hunger,
they will no longer thirst;
the sun will no longer strike them,
nor will any heat.
For the Lamb who is at the center of the throne
will shepherd them;
He will guide them to springs of living waters,
and God will wipe away every tear from their eyes." (Rev. 7:9–17)

The first observation to be made is the manner in which John's vision—at this point as at others throughout this letter—conflates at least two time frames: the tribulations and persecutions of the saints of God from the past and the future rectification of such injustices by the graciousness of God in establishing his consummated victory and reign forever. Yet the power of this particular vision is located in the way in which it represents the presence of God with and for his people even now—in their present of distress and disappointment in a delayed Parousia. God's presence, as disclosed in the presence of the Lamb with and for his people, serves to validate the hope of an even greater and more visible presence of God, as the victorious Lamb, who will provide his people with "springs of living water" while at the same time wiping "every tear from their eyes." And this vision of a genuine hope falls within the parameters of the narrative of the opening of the seals; that is to say, in the midst of these horrific occurrences comes another liturgical interlude, which is to be replicated by the community of faith on earth. It seems that genuine hope in the promised presence of God and God's future fulfillment of all that historically transpired in and through his Son, the Lamb of God, is sustained in the worship of God's people, when worship is centered in praise and thanksgiving for what God has already accomplished in Christ (i.e., salvation and the bestowal of graced freedom) and in anticipation of the final victory of all forces of destruction and the establishment of God's reign of creature and creation, this worshipful event strengthens hope in situations that would otherwise be unbearable and threaten one's faith.

That which remains unspoken and yet, at least by implication, is very much to the point in this passage, is the way in which graced freedom is also and at the same time reaffirmed (in this liturgical setting) as that which facilitates the form of obedience God desires, as obedience that emanates from a love which is, itself, freely given. The follower of Christ continues to find strength to endure the hardship depicted in each of the broken seals in the context of earthly worship (which obviously has its parallel in the worship of John's vision in heaven), in which the Presence of the Lamb is affirmed to be with and for his people, as Lord, in the midst of their distress; the Lamb bears the wounds of his sacrificial service for the sake of salvation, and his wounds disclose the level of this empathic regard for the suffering(s) of his children. There can be little doubt that the horrors, depicted by each of the first six seals being opened, could create or eventuate in an environment of emotional and spiritual "captivity." It is also possible that even for people of faith, a form of bondage to "bad faith" could develop, leading to the diminishment, if not loss, of a living hope in the promises of God and belief in the presence of the ruling Lamb. It would undermine and be just as destructive to the presence of graced freedom for the believer to renounce his or her faith in Christ, as it would be to abandon one's confessional conviction as a consequence of anxiety and mistrust regarding the credibility of God's promises, brought on by the tribulations and hardships dramatized in each of the six seals.

The Book of Revelation: Freedom for Humanity

Let us focus now on the opening words of this portion of the letter, in which the author writes: After this I looked, and there was a vast multitude from every nation, tribe, people, and language, which no one could number, standing before the throne and before the Lamb. In this passage we overhear a remarkable affirmation of the inclusivity of the final gathering of those who belong and submit to the Lordship of the Lamb! While the use of terms such as "nation, tribe, people, and language," could indicate some form of homogeneous grouping, such is highly doubtful; it is more likely symbolic of the inclusion of a multitude of peoples, gathered from every corner of the then-known world, to worship at the throne of the Lamb, which could also be said to symbolically parallel the event of Pentecost itself as the birth of the Church catholic. The heterogeneous nature of this grouping would also suggest that in the final hour all will come to bow before the Lamb of God, whose Lordship has been challenged in a variety of settings, over a variety of historical periods, and by a variety of political representatives. Having been "sheltered" by the Lamb from the otherwise devastating effects of persecution and trial, the Church is assured of ultimate victory and a joyful celebration of Christ's consummated victory in the courts of heaven itself; and they will come from "every nation, tribe, people, and language."

Those gathered at the foot of the Lamb's throne (that is, at least in part, a recognition of Christ's rightful rule) demonstrate their obedience in and through faithful worship and adoration of him who is rightful heir to sharing the throne of God. Like obedience, worship cannot be genuine when coerced (which distinguishes this worship from that of the emperor, as refusal to worship the emperor as *kurios* was always under threat of punishment), and those who are gathered here worship as an expression of the graced freedom, a freedom that has been actualized through the ministry of the Lamb, for which they offer praise and thanksgiving. It should also be noted that the designation (i.e., "every nation, tribe, people, and language") could be a symbolic representation of the whole of humanity, a mark of inclusivity; the restoration of graced freedom has empowered these saints to come through "the great tribulation" with a deeper sense of harmony among humanity than could ever have been established by the political machinations of any one Caesar or *kurios*. This graced freedom is for humanity in two senses: it is the gift of God in Christ to the whole of humanity as an act of love, forgiveness, and reconciliation, and it is the gift of the triumphant saints of Christ to humanity, which is in desperate need of agapic compassion and a serious call to repentance and reconciliation in

Christ. The capacity to remain faithful, despite the drastic consequences for those Christians who refuse to bend the knee to an earthly *kurios,* can only be possible within the framework of the graced freedom that serves as the foundation and inner substance of faith itself. Those who have washed their robes and made them white in the blood of the Lamb represent the faithful who have submitted in the fullness of their person to the Lordship of Christ over their life and death—as *kurios* of both—and provide an example to the earthly Church of a faith that is unflappable.

Chapters eight through eleven detail a number of different forms of tribulation, some of which mirror the plaques that occurred in Egypt prior to the exodus of the Hebrews, and the escalation of hardships on unbelievers and persecutions for the Church. However, after the story of Michael and the war that transpires in heaven itself (which culminates in the "dragon" or "Satan" being cast down to the earth), there is another liturgical interlude in which John hears a "loud voice" in heaven say:

> The salvation and the power
> and the Kingdom of our God
> and the authority of His messiah
> have now come,
> because the accuser of our brothers
> has been thrown out:
> the one who accuses them
> before our God day and night.
> They conquered him
> by the blood of the Lamb
> and by the word of their testimony,
> for they did not live their lives
> in the face of death.
> Therefore, rejoice, you heavens,
> and you who dwell in them!
> Woe to the earth and the sea,
> for the Devil has come down to you with great fury.
> Because he knows he has a short time. (Rev. 12:10–12)

It is difficult to say with absolute certainty whether this is intended as a narrative intended to dramatize the advent of Satan's reign, or intended to suggest the presence of Satan as the cause underlying the Church's experience with persecution, or again, is proposed anticipation of what will be at some point in the immediate or distant future. The reference to Satan as the "accuser" resonates with the prelude to the story of Job, but was, of course, not an uncommon term of referral to Satan, regardless of other associations.

The Book of Revelation: Freedom for Humanity

What is fascinating in the manner in which this passage asserts the current sovereignty of God and "His Messiah" even "now" and in the very midst of the Church's several hardships, which would undermine any claim by an earthly overload to absolute authority and any demand to be honored as "divine." The conquest of Satan has come by way of "the blood of the Lamb" and the "word of (the saints) testimony;" one thinks immediately of that well-known phrase of Tertullian: The blood of the martyrs is the seed of the Church! Such "testimony" (Greek *martyria*), and the fact that "they did not love their lives in the face of death," would imply a form of freedom well beyond that to be conferred in and through any one socio-political enterprise; it is only graced freedom that could establish the courage of faith necessary to commit one's life to martyrdom for the sake of the advancement of the gospel, the defeat of Satan, and the reconciliation of humanity in Christ, the Lamb. One should not interpret the phrase "they did not love their lives in the face of death" in any other way than as affirmation of their willingness to "lay down their life" for humanity, just as Christ had laid down his life for the forgiveness of sins and the salvation of humankind. I had a congregant who, at the tender age of nineteen, participated in the landing at Omaha beach, and suffered the loss of numerous friends on that day and in subsequent battles. When asked, "How did you manage to battle on?" he replied, "Our lives were dispensable for the much higher cause of defeating such evil, setting captives free, and establishing peace once more." If one does not hear resonance with the affirmation made in this passage (i.e., "they did not love their lives in the face of death"), then I am at a loss to provide a more graphic illustration of *martyria* outside the context of Christian faith as expressed in Revelation!

At this juncture we return to the second and third chapters of Revelation in order to analyze in brief each opening of the seven letters to the churches; it will be demonstrated that the threat to graced freedom came not only from external persecution of the church, but from dysfunctional faith and associated problems internal to the corporate church as the body of Christ as well as the individual believer. Throughout this letter the prophet John never loses sight of the necessary connection between the individual believer and the larger body of the church, as both are loved by Christ and both are accountable for the freedom and faith they've received as a gracious bestowal of divine love. In this way John avoids a problem that often arises in discussions of the contemporary church, where one focuses either too much on the corporate nature of the church or too much on the individual believer before God; either one diminishes the church as the

A Pastoral Proposal for an Evangelical Theology of Freedom

body of Christ in which (as Paul asserts) the individual, with his or her unique spiritual giftedness, and the corporate nature of the church as the one body of Christ, in both her local and global appearance, are essential to a catholic comprehension of the faith. This is, by way of preface, essential to understanding each of the seven letters to the churches of Asia; even so, we have limited space and will extract from each letter that which is central to our purpose.

> "Write to the angel of the church in Ephesus: the One who holds the seven stars in His right hand and who walks among the seven gold lampstands says: I know our works, your labor, and your endurance, and that you cannot tolerate evil. You have tested those who call themselves apostles and are not, and you have found them to be liars . . . But I have this against you: You have abandoned the love you had at first. Remember then how far you have fallen; repent and do the works you did at first." (Rev. 2:1–2, 3–5a)

One of the first items of importance to be noted is the way in which each of the seven addresses begins with the phrase "I know," which in every instance implies an intimacy of such knowledge, or said differently, Christ shares an intimate relationship with each of these churches so that what is being asserted is more than informational in character; it is, rather, knowledge that has either favorably or adversely affected the nature of the relationship shared. The way in which the "church" has conducted herself has a direct bearing on the welfare of the relationship shared in the Spirit of Christ, and therefore has direct bearing on the way in which the "church" witnesses (or gives "testimony"—*martyria*) to the "world" in which she is situated.

The church in Ephesus is addressed by the Lord of the cosmic order who also makes his presence known (by "walking") in and among the churches in the most ecumenical way; and while he acknowledges their faithful "labor" and "endurance" in a stand taken over against all forms of "evil," it is the absence of love that brings his displeasure. There is, evidently, nothing that is more central to the church than is agapic love, both the love of Christ as Lord and that same love expressed subsequently in ministries of grace. For the church in Ephesus all of the implicit spiritual "value" in her "labor" and "endurance" is drained to a minimum when compared with the love she once had for her Lord, which was at one time (i.e., "at first") the foundation for all that she was and all that she undertook in ministry. The centrality of "love" to the church cannot be underestimated, because it

The Book of Revelation: Freedom for Humanity

is only such "love" as that Christ has for and shares with the church that can sustain her life and ministry to the end; and "love" is as essential to salvation and obedience as graced freedom is to continuance in "love." In order for the church to be and remain an authentic community of freedom for humanity, she must nurture and nourish her life in the springs of that "love" Christ and Christ alone creates and sustains. "Write to the angel of the church in Smyrna: The First and the Last, the One who was dead and came to life, says: I know your affliction and poverty, yet you are rich. I know the slander of those who say they are Jews and are not, but are a synagogue of Satan. . . . Don't be afraid of what you are about to suffer. . . . Be faithful until death, and I will give you the crown of life" (Rev. 2:8–10).

The church in Smyrna is addressed by Christ as "the One who was dead and came to life," and is therefore Lord of both the dead and the living; this is the Christ whose Lordship is manifest in ever new beginnings, in bringing that which is to exist out of that which, for all intents and purposes, appears dead to the core. Note also the reference to this community of faith as one of "affliction (a code word for persecution) and poverty;" here is the church that can turn to Christ in genuine humility because she feels her need so keenly; dependence on Christ is not a weakness, but rather a manifestation of good faith. Since the church in Smyrna is under the Lordship of him who is "First and Last," she can be assured that her life is held in the providential grace of Christ as the author and finisher of their faith. Returning to the words of Christ in his Beatitudes, the church remembers that it is the "poor in spirit" and those who are "persecuted for righteous sake" who are blessed in that they know they must rely upon Christ and Christ alone for support and sustainability in the trials of this life. When the Lord encourages the church in Smyrna to remain "faithful until death," it is possibly an allusion to immanent persecution, but more likely an exhortation to remain faithful for the duration of life, both individual and corporate life. Apparently, the church in Smyrna has not lost "the love (it) had at first," but has nurtured the relationship with Christ in order to insure the continuance of such love, both within the church and, as a community of freedom for humanity, in its ministry to the world in which it is engaged each day. Graced freedom also enables the release or vice-grip hold on all material gain, knowing that even the most well-planned investment portfolio will not protect her from collapse, and will, perhaps, hasten the demise of the church through a diminishment of that form of spiritual dependence, on Christ and Christ alone, that is manifest in the image of "poverty." After all,

A Pastoral Proposal for an Evangelical Theology of Freedom

isn't it the Protestant faith that has lifted high the theological banner of the "sola" (i.e., *sola gratia, sola fide, sola Deo, sola Christus*, etc.)?

> "Write to the angel of the church in Pergamum: The One who has the sharp, double-edged sword says: I know where you live—where Satan's throne is! And you are holding onto to My name and did not deny your faith in Me, even in the days of Antipas. My faithful witness who was killed among you, where Santa lives . . . But I have a few things against you. You have some there who hold to the teaching of Balaam . . . to eat meat sacrificed to idols and to commit sexual immorality . . . you also have those who hold to the teachings of the Nicolatians. Therefore, repent!" (Rev. 2:12–16)

Amazingly the church in Pergamum is a church summoned to do battle by the Christ of the "sharp, double-edged sword!" Here is a church that is, by the acclamation of Christ himself, a community of faith living in that place which has become the realm of "Satan's throne," where, in fact, "Satan lives." And while, for the most part, the church in Pergamum has remained steadfast and stalwart in her faith and commitment to Christ, and thereby has demonstrated the continuance of graced freedom among her own, some have chosen the path of disobedience and bondage to Satan and his own religious rituals. Since the city of Pergamum (like other Roman cities of its time) was quite beautiful and had temples dedicated to Zeus, Athena, and the Emperor Augustus, it should not surprise us that John's vision would include a reference to this place as the home of "Satan's throne." There is much Christ commends in this church, but not the acts of disobedience that demonstrate a relinquishing of graced freedom in submission to Satan's own religious practices and ritualistic patterns, all of which sever merely to degrade humanity and the human soul. What makes this form of apostasy so appalling is that it is happening in an environment where the "battle lines" have obviously been clearly drawn (remember—this is where "Satan lives!"); when life is, for the most part, uninterrupted by the absurdity of abuse of persecution forsaking the faith and relinquishing one's freedom in Christ is another matter altogether. It is also important to note the Lord's reference to eating meat sacrificed to idols as an act of intimacy with those who were living lives contrary to that which Christ commands; in other words, this was not simply an act of defiance on the part of some members of the church in Pergamum, it was rather the intentional formation of relationships with those who practice idolatry. The church is most at risk when her flirtation with forbidden belief systems eventuates in the formation of relationships that demand she become other than Christ commands her to be and become; and graced freedom is most at risk of being relinquished when Christians flirt with spiritual practices that border on being idolatrous; then the church is no longer a community of freedom for humanity, but has turned inward and become self-serving.

> "Write to the angel of the church in Thyatira: The son of God, the One whose eyes are like a fiery flame and whose feet are like fine bronze, says: I know your works—your love, faithfulness, service, and endurance. Your last works are greater than your first. But I have this against you: You tolerate the woman Jezebel, who calls herself a prophetess and teaches and deceives My slaves to commit sexual immorality and to eat meat sacrificed to idols. I gave her time to repent, but she does not want to repent . . . I am the One who examines the minds and hearts, and I will give to each of you according to your works. I say to the rest of you in Thyatira, who do not hold to this teaching, who haven't known the deep things of Satan—as they say—I do not put any other burden on you." (Rev. 2:18–24)

The church in Thyatira receives what amounts to the lengthiest letter of the seven, in which the Christ who is "Son of God" and supreme Lord ("eyes like fiery flame" and "feet . . . like fine bronze"). Here again, as in some of the letters that have come before it, Thyatira is commended for her "love, faithfulness, service, and endurance." But there is also the reality that this church has tolerated some form of false faith and belief; there is a dysfunctional theology afoot in the church in Thyatira that has taken root and has already been the downfall of some Christians in that community. And even though the Lord has called this false "prophetess" to repentance, she has refused and remained in rebellion, causing others to join her in this misguided and immoral belief and practice. Here is a community of faith that has been divided by competing belief systems, one that is patently heretical and the other the orthodox faith founded on the gospel of Christ; a division that has led to broken communion and the entrenchment of some brethren standing over against others. It is also evident that those who have chosen to fall from grace and follow the prophetess have actually submitted to cultural persuasions, and the church as a whole has practiced the art of tolerance with those who have played the harlot with their Lord and his love. In line with our proposal, what we have here is a church in which some have sacrificed graced freedom for the sake of cultural accommodation, while others in the church have simply taken the road of least

A Pastoral Proposal for an Evangelical Theology of Freedom

resistance and tolerated such disobedient practice. A divided church, local and global, serves Christ haltingly because she is hampered by the drag of those for whom graced freedom has become passé. We will return to this image again and in greater detail in our next chapter.

> "Write to the angel of the church is Sardis: The One who has the seven spirits of God and the seven stars says: I know our works; you have a reputation for being alive, but you are dead. Be alert and strengthen what remains, which is about to die, for I have not found your works complete before My God. "Remember, therefore, what you have received and heard; keep it and repent . . ." But you have a few people in Sardis who have not defiled their clothes, and they will walk with Me in white, because they are worthy." (Rev. 3:1–4)

While each of the seven letters has something to contribute to the contemporary church, none is more dramatic than the words of Christ to the church in Sardis. What could possibly be more disturbing to a church than to receive word from her Redeemer that, while her reputation among those in the surrounding culture is that she is active, working to alleviate the injustices of the oppressed, and busy with all manner of "ministry," she was, in his eyes and in reality, dead! The warning resonates so clearly with the current trend in the church growth movement than one shutters to hear this admonition from the mouth of the Savior himself; so much of the "life" of the church is measured by how active is her membership and leadership, when such looks like life and is, in fact, the glossing of her spiritual demise. We would venture to guess that many pastors have known the frustration of being forced to enact "program upon program" in order to provide the appearance of vitality, when at the soul of the body spiritual life has been drained of its energy for genuine growth and maturity in Christ, in that which matters most. Such activity posing as "life" can also be a cover for a church in which graced freedom has waned and will, if the circumstance is not turned around, eventually become nonexistent.

One of the more captivating characteristics of this particular letter is the phrase spoken by Christ in which he says Remember . . . what you have received and heard; keep it and repent. The words (i.e., "received and heard") would imply the transmission of traditional doctrine and teaching with apostolic authority as it foundation; which would also suggest that one of the prevailing issues with the church in Sardis was the failure to retain the faith in good order and in the manner in which it has been taught

The Book of Revelation: Freedom for Humanity

them. Whatever one makes of the theological category of "tradition," one cannot overlook this word of Christ in which what has been "received" by the church must be retained and guarded in its transmission to generations of Christian believers; one of the major reasons for a church becoming confused in her identity and weakened in her witness to Christ could be traced directly to the failure to retain what had been "received" as apostolic truth and in faithfulness to the gospel. The retention of what has been "received" is also vital to the maintenance of graced freedom within both the individual believer and the community at large. In order for the church to be a community of freedom for humanity, she must have the ability to discern truth from fallacy in any believe system, her own included, and she must find the resources for engagement with humanity (for the sake of our Savior's call to "make disciples of all nations") she must know what it is she believes and what she does not believe to be true. Few things are move deleterious to the church than is her inability to articulate her own faith tradition, her own gospel, or own conviction regarding the supremacy and superiority of Christ to all other challengers to his Lordship.

> Write to the angel of the church in Philadelphia: The Holy One, the True One, the One who has the key of David, who opens and no one will close, and closes and no one opens says: I know your works. Because you have limited strength, have kept My word, and have not denied My name, looked, I have placed before you an open door that no one is able to close. . . . Because you have kept My command to endure, I will also keep you from the hour of testing that is going to come over the whole world to test those who live on the earth. . . . Hold on to what you have, so that no one takes your crown. (Rev. 3:7–11)

We begin our exploration of this letter by calling attention to the phrase "you have limited strength," and do so because like the church in Smyrna, this church reflects a kind of "poverty of spirit," a genuine acknowledgement of her need for the strength the Savior alone can provide. It is also evident that, like Smyrna, the church in Philadelphia is commended and not admonished; she has kept the "word" of Christ and has not "denied" his name – both of which indicate the retention of graced freedom and its subsequent obedience to the Lord. Interestingly this church is the only one in which Christ makes reference to that which he alone can "open" and "close," and in light of other uses of that same imagery in Revelation, one can reasonably assume that its meaning is the same: What Christ alone can "open" and "close" is the "door" or the way into heavenly realities (i.e., Christ is the "Way, Truth, and Life"), and for the church in Philadelphia this "door" is open in some perpetual sense, perhaps indicating the constant presence of Christ as Lord with and for the church, or it could be accessibility to the spiritual things of God in the power of the Holy Spirit. Regardless, it is an affirmation of the constancy of graced freedom being rewarded (if you will) with great spiritual strength to face whatever the church must face in the way of persecution or hardship. Most readers will recall that, in Greek, the word "Philadelphia" is a compound term meaning something like "love of the brother or brethren"; even so, such love extends well beyond the boundaries of the church's four walls, reaching out to a wounded and burdened humanity with the peace of the gospel message and the Christ it conveys. Should the church continue (by way of graced freedom) to obey Christ, by holding on to that which she already possesses in faith, she will never forfeit the "crown" of glory with which she has also already been blessed. There could be no more powerful and promising word to the church and her ongoing ministry of evangelism than to hear her lord affirm the constant openness of heaven to her cries for a fallen and often faithless humanity.

One more point before moving on: this entire letter to the church in Philadelphia is an affirmation of Christ's love for his people, his church, which is also evident in his gracious opening of the way into heaven and the presence of God. In return, what more gracious gift could the church then bring to a lost and languishing humanity, as humanity in bondage, than the proclamation of heaven having been opened (by and in Christ) to their deepest and greatest need for acceptance, forgiveness, mercy, and reconciliation. As Christ loved and loves his church, so the church, as a community of freedom for humanity, lives out such love in obedience to him who said "Go and make disciples of all nations."

> "Write to the angel of the church in Laodicea: The Amen, the faithful and true Witness, the Originator of God's creation says: I know your works, that you are neither cold nor hot. I wish you were cold or hot. So, because you are lukewarm, and neither hot nor cold, I am going to vomit you out of My mouth. Because you say, 'I'm rich; I have become wealthy and need nothing and you don't know that you are wretched, pitiful, poor, blind, and naked. . . . As many as I love, I rebuke and discipline. So be committed and repent." (Rev. 3:14–19)

The Book of Revelation: Freedom for Humanity

Of seven letters to the churches, this is the one that will be most familiar to the greatest number of readers. This is also the word of Christ which we suggest has the most notable application to the contemporary church, which has in so many ways become little more than "lukewarm" in her faith, evangelism, mission, and ministry to a broken and rebellious humanity. Here we have Christ's condemnation of the church in Laodicea for being far less than the powerful presence of graced freedom enables her to be and become; a church that has come to rely on everything other than her Lord; a church that thinks it is self-sufficient, needing "nothing" when, in fact, she needs everything essential to her continued life in Christ and as his body. Note should be given to Christ's personal reference in the heading to this letter, in which he stresses those characteristics that are patently lacking in the church in Laodicea – namely being "faithful" and a "true Witness" (recalling, as we should the Greek for witness: *martyria*). How, then, could the body of this same Christ prove to be less than faithful and a true witness to him and his gospel; only through the "lukewarm" character of disobedience. Where such disobedience is often associated with active engagement, we recognize in Christ's words an assertion that disobedience all too often has it origin in apathy, or what can be called "lazy faith."

The word of hope is found in Christ's promise: "As many as I love, I rebuke and discipline." Christ will not abandon his own, his church, even she is discovered to be resting on the laurels of her own accomplishments, or material sustenance, or personal charisma. But the church must also and always be prepared to be shaken out of the complacency and apathy by a Christ who, as Lord, calls her to repentance and the renewal of graced freedom for the purposes of obedience and more faithful service in his name. Christians can all too readily conform themselves to the surrounding culture and its tempting traditions of time spent enriching the self, at the expense of one's relationship with the living God, and eventually at the cost of one's soul. Apathy in worship attendance, in daily devotional practice, in tithing, in participation in the many ways of serving Christ in daily life, in the numerous obligations that are met only by free and faithful obedience, each and more are evident in the church that has become "lukewarm." Yet we all know how love is anything but lukewarm, its passion diminished to the point of a comprehensive and incessant yawn! Such is also the case with the love of Christ that is the substance of the church's mission thrust to a fallen humanity; if lukewarm, it simply lacks the passion to prevail in its pursuit of those evangelistic efforts that are for the eternal welfare of a hurting humanity, and therefore represent the very best characteristics of freedom for humanity.

Perhaps the contemporary church can hear the words of Christ in this passage and then acknowledge that any discipline or rebuke he has to bring to bear on her apathetic faith and practice of obedience is really an act of divine love, and a desire to restore her to that form of graced freedom which will energize her for a return to vibrant and faithful service to God and to the neighbor in need. While she is lukewarm, she is of no use to God or to humanity; Christ will not tolerate such condition for long, but the church upon hearing his call must, in his own words, be "committed and repent." Such repentance is the basis for the restoration of graced freedom, and such commitment is the manifestation of graced freedom restored for the purposes of service to Christ, his church, and a hurting humanity. It could be said that one of the reasons why the world itself, when looking at the contemporary church, yawns is that it witnesses a community awash in apathy, lukewarm in her love, and lusterless in her outreach of evangelism.

Having considered the seven letters to the seven churches of Asia we have hopefully provided some insight into those ways (other than in response to external persecution) by which the church surrenders her graced freedom from within the community of faith and by virtue of submission to temptations, whether they come in the clothing of heretical beliefs and associated practices or pressures to conform to cultural ideologies and other religions. Even though the contemporary church (at least in its North American context) is not threatened with persecution, there are any number of ways in which Satan still works to undermine graced freedom and the obedience it makes possible. We are convinced, in this manner, that Revelation still speaks to the church (as part of the canon) and not merely as a curiosity and fodder for "end-time" fanatics; the inspirational value of this letter is located in the numerous images employed to awaken the slumbering church to all manner of threat to graced freedom.

This chapter has already extended beyond that of the others, and perhaps even strained the patience of the reader, so let us bring this to a close with two further passages and comments of their relevance to graced freedom as freedom for humanity. The first of the final two passages to be considered is from the twenty-first chapter of Revelation:

> Then I saw a new heaven and a new earth, for the first heaven and the first earth had passed away, and the sea existed no longer. I also saw the Holy City, new Jerusalem, coming down out of

The Book of Revelation: Freedom for Humanity

heaven from God, prepared like a bride adorned for her husband. Then I heard a loud voice from the throne:
"Look! God's dwelling is
with men,
and He will live with them.
They will be His people,
and God Himself will be
with them and be their God.
He will wipe away every tear
from their eyes.
Death will exist no longer;
grief, crying, and pain with exist
no longer,
because the previous things
Have passed away." (Rev. 21:1–4)

Chapters 21 and 22 constitute the definitive word (or better, word) on the consummation of all John has witnessed and shared with the churches in this letter and by way of his prophetic office; the closing proclamation is a deliberate and victorious word. In this passage God's people are assured that in the end, the consummation as God has planned it, there will be great joy and the extension of graced freedom into eternity. All of those excruciating experiences associated with persecution and the internal battles of the church will find their resolution in the uninterrupted and immediate presence of God, who will be with them and be their God: which is to say, the reestablishment of full communion, uninterrupted by the paradox of sin and its consequences, not with humanity in general, but with the "people of God", or to paraphrase the language of the apostle Paul, "Jew and Greek, slave and free, male and female!" God's presence is not unlike the "tabernacle" presence of the wilderness wandering, or the Holy of Holies in the Temple, of the Word made flesh in Christ; this is an intimate and therefore relational presence, a reestablishment of faith's first freedom, in the giftedness of the covenantal relationship.

This passage proclaims the finalization of all those sufferings associated with a creation and creature in bondage to sin—Death, grief, crying, and pain—all have now come to an end, and what remains is the joyous freedom of a relationship of renewal, recreation and consummated redemption. The graced freedom necessitated under the dominion of sin is no longer demanded in this setting of God's absolute Lordship, of God's intimate and immediate presence, of God's gracious and compassionate care for his people. If it can be asserted, as we believe it can and must be, that "home" represents that place where freedom breathes in the clear air of relational love, loyalty, and devotion to the welfare of the other, then this passage symbolizes God's establishment of the earth as the "home" for God-self and for God's people, where freedom is evident in the fulfillment of covenantal connectedness and all worship returns to that place which represents the center of the cosmic order itself, that is, the "new Jerusalem."

If we consider this incredible passage in light of the contemporary setting of the holy city of Jerusalem, in which, even as we write these words (November 26, 2012), there continues to be bloodshed, brokenness, and regrettably, far too much "bad blood" between the three major faiths tracing their origins back to father Abraham, it is evident that graced freedom—for the Jew, Christian, and Muslim—is threatened by political machinations and social stigmas of which only sin could be the cause. John's vision assures us that God's time is coming when graced freedom will, itself, be the order of the day and land, and make it presence and power felt in that there will be nothing save the willing and generous exchange of God's grace, expressed in an unencumbered freedom for humanity; or said differently, freedom for the enlargement and enrichment of human communion and among a diversity of nations and peoples, symbolically represented at present by the designations of "Jew, Christian, and Muslim."

We conclude this exploration and exposition with a text we would claim summarizes the vision John received, as one in which all that presently thwarts and threatens the expression of graced freedom, as freedom for humanity (again as both God's intended gift and established order in creation, and as the expression of faith among believers, followers of the slaughtered Lamb), will end and God will graciously consummate the full measure of promise revealed in Christ Jesus in God's complete reign:

> I did not see a sanctuary in (the new Jerusalem), because the Lord God the Almighty and the Lamb are its sanctuary. The city does not need the sun or the moon to shine on it, because God's glory illuminates it, and its lamp is the Lamb. The nations will walk in its light and the kings of the earth will bring their glory into it . Each day its gates will never close because it will never be night there. They will bring the glory and honor of the nations into it. Nothing profane will ever enter it: no one who does what is vile or false, but only those written in the Lamb's book of life. (Rev. 21:21–24)

What a glorious vision of the consummation of all that was formally witnessed in the life, ministry, death, resurrection and ascension of Jesus

Christ! With such a profound vision in hand the church in any and every generation need not tremble in the face of even the most dire tribulation, knowing that this promise of God will come to completion, just as John's vision has presented it, and as a historical reality. The "when" is muted by the great antiphonal sound of the proclamation itself, and the believer can rest secure in the knowledge (recall Christ's "I know" as the first word in each of the seven letters) that the certainty of this vision becoming reality is no less than the present situation of pain or distress of any kind whatsoever; this is the promise of the God who has always remained faithful to the fulfillment of his Word, whenever and wherever it has been spoken to God's people. This vision itself enables one to breathe freely, even with the scars of captivity still evident on one's physical frame, or even on one's heart and soul; it is a vision of a "city" in which there is nothing that will cause diversions, disregard for the needs of the neighbor, or deliberate disobedience and the resulting fragmentation of communal harmony. Here, graced freedom finds its fullest expression in that peace, *shalom*, which is the hallmark of God's eternal love and good will for both creature and creation, and in particular for those who have remained faithful as covenant partners.

In this consummated "city" only God and God's Lamb are acknowledged to reign supreme, by every nation and former king, who willingly and joyfully brings all of the richest treasures and glory of the former kingdom, to place in humble adoration at the foot of the throne of God. The "gates" are never closed because there is no internal or external threat to the harmony of the "city" and the welfare of its residents; this is freedom in the fullest measure of grace, unencumbered by risk to misuse or even abuse, and please notice that humanity is the beneficiary, and in particular, those who belong (covenantal commitment) to the Lamb. This can be called a "Christian" city only to the extent that each and every resident is in Christ, with Christ, and willing to worship (as free and faithful service) Christ alone among the so-called 'lords' of the earth; in fact, there are no lords, since all have submitted to the reign of the Savior in the full glory of God's kingdom on earth (i.e., they will bring the glory and the honor of the nations into [the city]). In the complete absence of all that is malicious and destructive there can only be the presence of graced freedom in fullness and such freedom for humanity, as a consummated reality, represents the "whole" of humankind (symbolized by the Church as *oikumene*! And so we now move forward, from this prophetic word and glorious letter of hope, to the next chapter and our presentation of the ecumenical significance of graced freedom for the Church as a whole.

6

The Ecumenical Characteristics of Graced Freedom

AT FIRST BLUSH THE suggestion that graced freedom, as it has been defined and used thus far in this essay, would seem anomalous to the complexities of ecumenical conversations among those confessional bodies engaged in this vital concern for greater visible unity, the irregularity is due more to the novelty of the proposal than it is to the particular use of the concept itself. While there have been innumerable references to the centrality of the concept of freedom, as more generally understood, to the entire process of dialogue and engagement along ecumenical lines, this is—at least to our knowledge—the first time the effort has been made to place graced freedom at the center of ecumenicity as it applies to each and all of the participating confessional bodies.

In this chapter we contend that there has been progress along the lines of ecumenicity as a consequence of and as witness to the reality of graced freedom among participants. Moreover, we assert that there can only be further progress in ecumenical engagements to the extent that participants now recognize graced freedom as the spiritual resource, given and sustained by the Holy Spirit alone, which enables greater receptivity to learning fruitfully from the traditions of other participants, without the requirement of reciprocation as prelude to such receptivity. Furthermore, it is graced freedom, in the fullest reality of expression, which not only makes such receptivity possible, but will also and at the same time energize any further movement in the direction of greater visible unity.

The Ecumenical Characteristics of Graced Freedom

The presence and commonality of graced freedom among those who belong to Christ as members of his body, the Church catholic, is the foundation upon which there can be an open and honest meeting, with exploration of, and dialogue on those issues that continue to divide us. All participating parties must remain receptive to the manner in which their own position can, and perhaps should, be modified in light of what is learned from the others in the process of open exploration; of course, this implies a certain degree of reciprocity, so that the conversation is truly multilateral and not simply unilateral. We are not advocating any form of freedom from what some might call the constraints of one's own commitment to elements of his or her tradition and/or a particular confessional position. Rather, we are advocating an understanding of and appreciation for graced freedom as that spiritual reality which facilitates the capacity to be free for openness, and therefore receptivity, to those elements of another's confessional position that promise to enrich one's own, and freedom from the inability or even unwillingness to engage in such dialogic exploration, due to an unhealthy attachment to elements of one's own confessional position and commitments.

In his epistle to the Ephesians the apostle Paul wrote: "For by grace you are saved through faith, and this is not from yourselves; it is God's gift—not from works, so that no one can boast. For we are His creation—created in Christ Jesus for good works, which God prepared ahead of time so that we should walk in them" (Eph. 2:8–9). This passage is classically employed for ecumenical discussion on justification and salvation. However the same general assertion of this passage could be rightly declared of graced freedom as a gift of God in Christ Jesus, conferred upon all Christians, so that their obedience is solely the by-product of *agapic* love associated with such freedom in Christ, and they can generously "walk" in the "good works" God intended as a manifestation of the presence of graced freedom in their lives. That which separates Christian brothers and sisters across confessional and denominational lines, while never to be treated with disregard or simplistic dismissals—as though such weighty matters were in actuality inconsequential—must be framed within the context of the unconditional freedom we have been given in Christ, to become and remain vulnerable to modifications and even changes in our own doctrinal and confessional positions, noting that which is deficient in our own traditions, yet vibrantly present in that of the other. The old "bug-a-boo" of leveling out the field of ecumenical dialog to the "lowest common denominator" in order to establish a basis for greater visible unity is simply not in question; no one, with even a minimal comprehension of the complexity of ecumenical decision making, would advocate such an absurdity at this point in time! We are arguing for a more proactive or purposeful exploration of the degree to which participants in any ecumenical encounter are engaging in this critical effort with consciousness of and respect for the opportunities made possible by way of the commonality of graced freedom; attentiveness, which is essential to genuine and fruitful dialog, must also and always imply receptivity as well, or one is simply engaging in a unilateral conversation, without benefit to either party so engaged.

Almost from its inception the ecumenical "movement" has embraced two biblical passages as foundational to its proceedings and process of dialog among representatives of the various confessional and denominational bodies engaged: One is a line from the passage of what has often been called the "High Priestly Prayer" of Christ (i.e., "May they all be one, as You Father are in Me, and I am in You. May they also be one in Us, so that the world may believe you sent Me" [John 17:21–22]) and the other also from John's Gospel (i.e., "But I have other sheep that are not of this fold; I must bring them also, and they will listen to my voice. Then there will be one flock, one shepherd" [John 10:16]). Both passages imply—the one as a prayerful petition and the other as stated intent of our Lord—that the greater visible unity we seek can only be achieved through a profound obedience, such that we can no longer rationalize our divisions in the face of these startlingly candid words of our Lord Christ. This is not to assert that we must ignore the long and painful history that began in or around the eleventh century and has continued since to see divisions beyond those of East and West, leading to our present situation (which, we believe, the apostles and early church fathers would have found deplorable—to say the least) in which divisions continue to manifest a brokenness in the Church catholic, even as ecumenical initiatives continue to be considered. We are merely wanting to raise the red flag of caution that such sustained divisions (continued causes of division which could and should have been resolved by now, but for an element of inexplicable resistance) could also be understood to form a profound and entrenched disobedience (*de facto*) to that which is the expressed desire of the Lord Christ for his body, the Church catholic (*de jure*), and therefore constitutes persistence in sin that causes great grief to the Holy Spirit. In line with our own purpose in this essay we would also contend that these sustained divisions (which continue to fester in Christ's body) bring into question (before the eyes of the world) the presence and reality of graced freedom in the life of the Church as the people of God.

One of the more important reasons behind the pressing desire for greater visible unity is stated in the prayer of our Lord when he said, "so that the world may believe you sent Me." It may be that the Church catholic has become so preoccupied with her own survival in a world cultural setting in which she is seldom perceived as "relevant" to the "felt needs" of a "world come of age" (to borrow a phrase from Dietrich Bonhoeffer) that this expressed prayerful petition of Christ has been forgotten. It needs to be said, however, that the churches in North America have a particular responsibility in light of the fact that, almost from the "birth of the nation," they have benefited from a generous and expansive liberality, seldom if ever afforded the Christian church in any other setting; this setting enables churches in North America to more freely engage in ecumenical pursuits—freed as they are from the encumbrances of persecution, political suppression, or other forms of socio-political restrictions. Perhaps the greatest encumbrance to churches in this setting has been religious pluralism and an effective secularization, together with the church's tendency to become acculturated to the expressed needs of spiritual "seekers" and others who have little interest in commitment to confessional positions. All too often in this same environment the freedom associated with the gospel is little more than a mirror image of that form of freedom associated with the historical development of the nation, and therefore is seen to be the safeguard of a stalwart individualism, where independence and self-reliance are the "order of the day," and which tends to then undervalue if not undermine the importance of the essential context in which graced freedom thrives (i.e., the Church as the Body of Christ).

Many have indicated that the ecumenical endeavor has been at an impasse for more than a decade, yet we assert that the genuine thrust for continued efforts at greater visible unity must begin—at least in part—with an acknowledgement of the centrality of such unity in the Church's task of evangelism. Said differently; the "world" will most likely raise serious questions and have severe doubts regarding the actuality of "reconciliation" (as the accomplished work of Christ for which he "came into the world"), when the Church catholic herself continues to be damaged by divisions that seem to suggest her own inability to be "reconciled" within her own confessional community of faith (i.e., the Church catholic). We will turn our attention below to one of the most important conciliatory documents to have been issued by the Faith and Order commission of the World Council of Churches (i.e., often referred to as the Lima document, better known as *Baptism, Eucharist, and Ministry*, hereafter *BEM*). For the moment, however, we do not think it hyperbolic at all to stress how the time has been too long in coming for greater visible unity, advancing beyond what was accomplished and resulted in *BEM*, so that the "world" will clearly see the Church catholic as a body in which reconciliation is the life-blood of her heart and the fresh winds of the Holy Spirit the breath that animates her soul. In its chapter on baptism the *BEM* states the importance of what we are asserting when it affirms the following: "When baptismal unity is realized in the one, catholic, apostolic Church, a genuine Christian witness can be made to the healing and reconciling love of God. Therefore, our one baptism into Christ constitutes a call to the churches to overcome their divisions and visibly manifest their fellowship."[1] We also assert that graced freedom alone establishes the power by which the Church catholic can and will enter into greater appreciation for and realizations of the hope generated by the Lima document (*BEM*).

One of the more insightful lines of this document comes in the paragraph with is titled, "Participation in Christ's Death and Resurrection," and serves to reinforce the magnitude of our theme in the present essay, when it asserts that "those baptized are no longer slaves to sin, but are free."[2] To some readers this affirmation may seem patently obvious, yet in the context of a document intended to serve the interests of furthering visible unity among churches, and in light of our purpose in this essay, this affirmation of a biblically-based theme takes on extreme importance. The "freedom" conferred is as much a gift of God in the power of the Holy Spirit as is faith and the sacrament itself, and the church practices this sacrament in full obedience to the command of her Lord, and in full knowledge of the fact that this particular freedom is freedom "from" sin and "for" obedience. The fullest expression of this graced freedom comes in the eventual and personal confession of faith in Christ as Lord and Savior, and as a further step in the desire to express full devotion to Christ in and through the fellowship, worship life, and mission of Christ's Body. The baptized member of the Body of Christ should not be made to feel that his or her "home" is limited to the local congregation, but that this graced freedom, which is shared with brothers and sisters in the Church catholic, assures a commonality of

---

1. *Baptism, Eucharist and Ministry*, 3.
2. Ibid., 2.

The Ecumenical Characteristics of Graced Freedom

faith, hope, and love, evident in the whole Church, and that such freedom (which is always and only conferred by God in the power of the Holy Spirit) is the key that opens the portals of fellowship with all Christians—regardless of their present confessional convictions.

Living in such freedom it is also essentially an imperative of faith upon all and each who have been baptized and confessed faith in Christ as Lord, to participate in the pursuit of ecumenical interests, not merely as a stated ministry and objective of any one official church hierarchy or body, but as his or her obedient service to the Lord whose High Priestly Prayer states his most profound desire for such unity in faith, hope, and love. To treat the advance of visible unity as though it were little more than a concern reserved for those hierarchs and theologians who tend to "dabble" in such abstractions, is to disclose a fraudulent faith, a faith that fails to hear the Prayer of Christ as a command to his people as well! With graced freedom we are each of us and all of us together called of Christ to extend ourselves in vulnerability and in all good faith to pursue the furtherance of visible unity, in testimony (to the world) of the power of reconciliation in the Spirit, and as a supremely indicative feature of what it means to be baptized into the "one Body of Christ."[3] In this fashion the Church catholic also testifies to the centrality of her purpose as that of "evangelism" in the fullest and richest sense of the term (i.e., in fulfillment of Christ's command in Matt. 28:16–20), and in her compassionate care for a fallen and fracture humanity to bear vibrant witness to the reality of God's coming kingdom of unhindered freedom: "Baptism initiates the reality of the new life given in the midst of the present world. It gives participation in the community of the Holy Spirit. It is a sign of the kingdom of God and of the life of the world to come. Through the gifts of faith, hope and love, baptism has a dynamic which embraces the whole of life, extends to all nations, and anticipates a day when every tongue will confess that Jesus Christ is Lord to the glory of God the Father."[4] Where some might see this as but another form of Christian "triumphalism," we advocate that it is the essential reality of the Church catholic to enact such graced freedom by an embracing the whole (*oikumene*) of humanity—and yes the world—in the kindness

---

3. "As they grow in the Christian life of faith, baptized believers demonstrate that humanity can be regenerated and liberated. They have a common responsibility, here and now, to bear witness together to the Gospel of Christ, the Liberator of all human beings. The context of this common witness is the Church and world" (ibid, 4).

4. Ibid., 3.

of Christ and in the desire to achieve that form of harmony which is both proleptic reality and a foretaste of God's coming kingdom.

The last sentence underscores the eschatological dimension of graced freedom as God's initially granted and forwardly sustained gift to the Church catholic but not for the purposes of liberation from the constraints of temptation and sin alone; we comprehend the full measure of this divinely-bestowed freedom when it is understood to anticipate the eschatological fulfillment of the harmoniousness of all interrelationships, both individual and more global, witnessed in the person and work of Christ. In other words, we see the actualization of the fulfillment of graced freedom in its proleptic characteristic as anticipatory of the eventual redemption of all things within the *oikumene* at the level of cosmic order; what is evident in the Church catholic (and therefore in the life of each believer) of graced freedom today, is the microcosm of what will one Day be the universal establishment of God's reign of freedom and grace, as the macrocosmic reality for all to see and know. Graced freedom, as freedom for humanity, is intended to establish in the world as we presently live it, the basis for the eventual (the inevitable) establishment of God's kingdom throughout; in this sense all ecumenical endeavors are essentially eschatological.

If baptism is the fundamental sacrament of Christian unity, then it is equally true to assert that the Eucharist is the communal celebration of thanksgiving in which the Church catholic rejoices—as the people of God—for that which has been accomplished in Christ and for the promised fulfillment of the same in God's coming kingdom. Each and every celebration of this sacramental feast is a foretaste of that final and ultimately fulfilling festival of God's eternal reign; each Eucharist is a sign of the renewal God has established in Christ, a renewal that awaits completion in God's coming kingdom. Even though Christian communities continue to break this bread and share this cup in unacceptable divisions, each and every celebration in each and every local congregation is symbolic of the unity we presently share in Christ as one Body (see 1 Cor. 10:16–18), and thereby bears testimony to the fulfillment of this feast and the promised reconciliation of all God's people in the coming kingdom of God where unity will no longer be the "thorn in the flesh" of Christ's Body! Whenever and wherever this sacrament of bread and cup is celebrated, the Church catholic is bearing witness to the profound harmony that can be established through the faithful employment of graced freedom:

The Ecumenical Characteristics of Graced Freedom

> As it is entirely the gift of God, the eucharist brings into the present age a new reality which transforms Christians into the image of Christ and therefore makes them his effective witnesses. The eucharist is precious food for missionaries, bread and wine for pilgrims on their apostolic journey. The eucharistic community is nourished and strengthened for confessing by word and action the Lord Jesus Christ who gave his life for the salvation of the world. As it becomes one people, sharing the meal of the one Lord, the eucharistic assembly must be concerned for gathering also those who are at present beyond its visible limits, because Christ invited to his feast all for whom he died. Insofar as Christians cannot unite in full fellowship around the same table to eat the same loaf and drink from the same cup, their missionary witness is weakened at both the individual and the corporate levels.[5]

The Eucharist shows forth to the world the desire of God for all to gather at the table banquet of his Son in the coming kingdom; as surely as the Lord God desires that all come to a saving knowledge of his Son in and through the proclamation of the gospel and the gift of grace, so God has established the sacramental meal as a communion in and with Christ, which, under the powerful influence of the Holy Spirit, is also directed as witness to the world in which there continues to be far too much disharmony—and disorder of the kind that carries the scent of sin's disgrace—of the reconciliation God holds out to a weary world, worn-down as it is by sin and suffering. Breaking the bread and sharing in the cup are sacramental exemplifications of the power of graced freedom to renew formally ruptured relationships and to provide for the nourishment of that form of Christ-like character that can and will empty itself in service to and for the other; each Eucharist reminds the world that there is a higher form of freedom—as the freedom of faith established in and by Christ Jesus—a freedom for humanity. At the Eucharist the Church catholic, while practicing the *anamnesis* of the sacrament also becomes a community in which graced freedom is made present the spiritual reality of the Lord who creates and confers such freedom, and awaits the awakening of a slumbering world to the joy and fulfillment that can be theirs by embracing graced freedom and living a life of joyful obedience to him who came into this world "not to be served, but to serve, and to give His life—a ransom for many" (Mark 10:45):

> Reconciled in the eucharist, the members of the body of Christ are called to be servants of reconciliation among men and women and

---

5. Ibid., 15.

witnesses of the joy of resurrection. As Jesus went out to publicans and sinners and had table-fellowship with them during his earthly ministry, so Christians are called in the eucharist to be in solidarity with the outcast and to become signs of the love of Christ who lived and sacrificed himself for all and now gives himself in the eucharist.[6]

In this fashion the community of faith demonstrates the presence and power of graced freedom in obedience to the crucified-risen-reigning Lord Christ, in self-giving for the sake of the enrichment of the other—the neighbor in need, and does so not merely from a position of obligation, but as an enactment of that divine love that had first grasp his or her life (i.e., "We love because He first loved us" [1 John 4:19]). This is one of the clearest manifestations of graced freedom eucharistically enlarging the parameters of agapic love beyond that normally associated with members of the community of faith, as shared with brothers and sisters, and expended freely and joyfully on the sojourner, the stranger, and the one whose name and face are unfamiliar—and yet are recognized as mysteriously bearing the countenance of Christ himself! The Eucharistic celebration is, therefore, a liturgical event in which the whole of humanity is held before the love of God in Christ and welcomed to enjoy the fruits of graced freedom in Christ and as anticipation of complete freedom in God's coming kingdom.

Regarding the ecumenical endeavor, the traditions of the Protestant faith that recognize and celebrate only two sacraments (i.e., Baptism and the Eucharist), continue to maintain an intimate ecumenical connection to those confessional communities (Roman Catholic and Pan-Orthodox in particular) that recognize and celebrate these two, and other, sacraments as well. Each time either of the two sacraments are celebrated—regardless of the setting in which they are practiced—the essential nature of the church as one, holy, catholic, and apostolic is once again affirmed. To whatever degree possible, the world is also reminded in these two sacraments of the love of God which has embraced the whole of life (*oikumene*) in and with the gift of Jesus Christ his Son, and has set his seal, the mark of his graced freedom (as actual and anticipatory), on the whole of the cosmic order. God's love extends well beyond the boundaries of the Church catholic to the entire *oikumene*, and therefore, whoever celebrates the sacraments of Baptism and Eucharist does so with the whole Church, as an affirmation of the unity we presently share, and as a proleptic sign of an ever expanding push toward greater visible unity as well.

6. Ibid., 14–15.

The Ecumenical Characteristics of Graced Freedom

The ecumenical endeavor provides one of the most potent symbols of the reality of graced freedom, for both inter-relational dialogue within the Church catholic, seeking wider expressions of convergence, and the relationship between the Church and the world, to the degree that churches are enabled to cross over confessional boundaries (responsibly and respectfully) while preserving the liberty essential to the continued maintenance of those confessional elements unique to defining any one given body of believers. In this time of globalization, where the efforts to achieve greater visible unity must take into consideration all of the social, political, and even economic factors impacting the process of ecumenicity itself, the reality of graced freedom becomes all the more important; while the Church catholic is not a "democratic" institution, she survives and expands through those evangelistic endeavors that are funded by the reality of graced freedom, which also serves as the fuel of her every attempt to advance visible unity. And it is just because the Church catholic is everywhere and always a community meant to be "in" though not "of" the world, that the Church catholic, in the spirit of ecumenicity, can testify most strikingly to the authentic liberation from every form of bondage (social, political, economic, and spiritual) in the world, demonstrating her essential nature as an ecumenical body, praying and working to advance freedom for humanity in every corner of the globe.

An evangelical theology of freedom, when framed within the context of ecumenical concerns, will—as has been true for every concern addressed throughout the history of the ecumenical endeavor—come to the fullest understanding of centrality of graced freedom to any concept of unity, from a careful and critical study of the biblical testimony to the formation and maintenance of the community of faith (Israel and the Church) as covenantal communities, established at the initiative of God and maintained by virtue of the presence and empowerment of the Holy Spirit. Both Scripture and Tradition must play an active role in the comprehension of how it is that the Lord God has (historically) maintained the community of faith, in a variety of settings and from within an equally diverse number of cultural environments, only through the maintenance of a freedom that transcends all differences and divisions, binding the covenantal community in a unity that can, itself, be maintained only with the enrichment and enlargement of graced freedom. Therefore the development of any ministry or initiative intended to advance the cause of visible unity must articulate, in the clearest terms possible, the crucial nature of graced freedom and its implication(s) for the proposed ministry; in other words, the reality, obligations, and accountability to obedience that are common to graced freedom must be stated, and find convergence, among the confessional parties involved with the conciliar agreement in any one ecumenical endeavor. Whenever the ecumenical concern being addressed fails to touch on the effect such judgment will have on the Church catholic and her witness to the world of the reality of graced freedom, as the God-conferred blessing that has made all reconciliation possible, the effort must be made to bear testimony to that same truth so that this grace is seen to be a freedom for humanity.

Ecumenicity, in the broadest sense of the term, should generate interest in further biblical and theological research and shared table talk on an issue of importance such as the topic of graced freedom—as freedom for humanity. Together with other crucial issues facing the whole of the ecumenical endeavor, this could be another topic to garner the giftedness and insights of biblical and theological scholars, contributing another dynamic to the ongoing effort to advance greater visible unity. Our position has been to merely provide some initial insights, from the vantage point of pastoral theology in a local congregation, and from membership within a denominational body (i.e., the United Church of Christ) that has, from its inception, been active in ecumenical engagements. We also see developments in both Church catholic and world that appear to necessitate a more purposeful—even though provisional—examination of graced freedom, where human life, as created *imago Dei*, is valued and called to live in such a way that this divinely conferred freedom is both acknowledged and revered as God's gift and as the basis for the enrichment of harmonious existence among humans and across every boundary that presently serves to separate them—geopolitical, economic, confessional in character, and more broadly religious in orientation. In a world in which the euphemism of "global village" has become common parlance, focus on and increased appreciation for the biblical-theological category of graced freedom, as a reality conferred by God, becomes even more essential to the establishment of relationships devoid of hatred, division, and disharmony. Whether it be through the ministry of the Faith and Order or Life and Work Commission of the World Council of Churches, taking-up the central issue of the significance of graced freedom would, we believe, serve to strengthen any endeavor to advance visible unity and to provide ministries of universal service to a broken and disharmonious humankind, which will justly represent the promise of God's coming kingdom.

The Ecumenical Characteristics of Graced Freedom

The brevity of this chapter, when compared to any of the others, should not be misconstrued to represent a measurement of our appreciation for the importance of graced freedom to the entire ecumenical enterprise of our lack of appreciation for those who have devoted and continue to devote so much of their time, energy, and prayerful creativity to this endeavor. We would remind the reader that we see the present work to be an essay and not a book, in the sense that in a book we would hope to expand the entire argument well beyond the limits set by an essay. As with my previously published essays, I offer this proposal as the basis for further dialogue and debate on both the nature of graced freedom and the significance of this theological category for the development a more extensive or expansive study. Since we offer this as a beginning—an initial and respectful response to what we understand to be a "hope" expressed the late Dr. Karl Barth—by God's grace, we can anticipate that there will be ample opportunity in the future to expand on the theme of this chapter and the entire theme of the essay itself. For now, we turn to our final chapter, presenting what are also some provisional and brief observations on the prospects of this proposal for pastoral ministry.

Conclusion

Prospects for Pastoral Ministry

THE PROSPECTS OF AN evangelical theology of graced freedom for aspects of pastoral ministry are many, so we must—due to the constraints of this essay format—highlight only those that are of greatest significance to the realities of pastoral service in the Church catholic. We stress that this is pastoral ministry in the Church catholic, because we are of the conviction that each and every act of pastoral ministry done at the local level of service has a consequential impact on the larger ecumenical body of Christ. This is not intended to be mere hyperbole; we are basing this conviction on more than thirty years of service in ordained pastoral ministry in service at the local level of congregational life, and have witnessed the numerous ways in which the services in Christ performed at one local level of congregational life can, and often does, have resonance throughout the wider Church as well. The Protestant pastor, the priest of the Roman Catholic, Anglican, or Orthodox church, visit the sick, celebrate Eucharist with the homebound, bury the dead, care for the bereaved, counsel the lost and languishing, and attend to countless other forms of pastoral care; in the process they mirror the very same compassion of Christ, shepherding of the flock, preaching, teaching, and provision of spiritual direction. All of these forms of pastoral care—regardless of the confessional position of the pastor holding office—would not be possible without the empowerment of graced freedom.

On any number of occasions throughout this essay we have stated our observation that, as a generality, contemporary Christians have liberty (i.e., a sense of self-governance, self-assertion, and individuation), but seldom demonstrate the presence of graced freedom in their lives. In fact, the church/Church often appears to resonate more with its socio-cultural

Conclusion

surroundings than it does the biblical and theological reality of the *ekklēsia*, as the people of God. Nowhere is this more evident than in the significant changes that have been made to a number of ministries in the church/Church. For example, worship has in many instances and settings been transformed into something just shy of entertainment; tricky and gimmicky aphorism are used on church signs to attract otherwise indifferent passersby; and fewer and fewer ordained clergy (mostly in Protestant settings) wear the traditional clerical collar and accompanying dress; and many worship services now include "praise hymns" sounding more like contemporary music than the traditional hymnody. Some of these changes (and others) are a welcome relief from the all-too-often stagnant atmosphere of much of worship (again, at least in Protestant communities); nevertheless, this same environment is not favorable for the necessary in-depth form of preaching and liturgical confirmation the promotion and nurturing of graced freedom demands.

The one holding pastoral office is fundamentally responsible, and frankly, under obligation by virtue of the vows of ordination, to bring about the needed reversal of such changes—and in particular regarding the "work of the people of God," that is, worship.

What pastor has not encountered the strong resistance that often accompanies any move in the direction of change, even when such change is, essentially, a return to earlier practices and therefore not necessarily novel. Yet, such resistance can, itself, be indicative of the absence of graced freedom and therefore disobedience to the directive guidance of the Holy Spirit; members of the church/Church often take positions on critical issues facing them as if such issues could be meaningfully resolved by mere vote and majority approval. Our point here is that graced freedom would be manifest in that community of faith in which the members would make all crucial decisions via the fine (and biblical) art of conciliarism, allowing the Holy Spirit to guide the community in the process of making difficult decisions by way of a conciliar conclave of members who are then representative of the diversity of the whole body. When done with attention to the way in which graced freedom functions to establish an environment in which obedience to the perceived movement of the Holy Spirit is imperative, critical decisions could be handled with a much finer finesse than is commonly experienced in local congregations, and in this manner the local congregation also demonstrates her real character as *ekklēsia*.

Conclusion

The reclamation of the centrality of graced freedom to every aspect of the worship life, mission, and ministry of the *ekklēsia* is imperative in our contemporary situation, where the church/Church has been willing to replace the traditional forms of worship and ministry with those informed more by social and cultural expressions and ideological concepts; in the process the *ekklēsia* has been the sole fatality. With such changes the church/Church has come to look more like another voluntary organization, with a religious tint, but having little of the substantive biblical-theological *paradosis* that has been the life-blood of the *ekklēsia* ever since Pentecost, as evidenced in the apostolic epistles and those of the early theologians. It has been suggested that this tendency to abandon "traditional" practices of spiritual nurture and enrichment, in favor of those that better suit the felt-needs of contemporaries, is indicative of openness, tolerance, and liberality. But we would contend that what is gained, in terms of numbers of participants in such communities, cannot compensate for what is lost, in terms of the richness of those biblical and theological traditions in which graced freedom has been nurtured, enriched, and enlarged. The position of those who would argue that this acculturated Christianity is the only way to assure the survival of the church/Church are correct, but only to the extent that what survives is but a shadow of the *ekklēsia*, which is born, sustained, and upheld by the Spirit of him who is both Lord and Christ!

The pastor who preaches, teaches, and provides spiritual direction with the intent of enriching the gift of graced freedom among those members of the *ekklēsia* under his or her care will soon than later discover the overall worship life, ministry, and mission of that congregation growing in those ways to have always been essential to the gospel of Jesus Christ; not "numbers of participants"—as that has seldom, if ever, been of concern to the Lord (simply read your Scriptures, where the remnant is always central)—but the intensification and enlargement of obedience to the Lord, as evidence of graced freedom, is paramount. We need not apologize for retention of those traditions that seem to some "outdated" and even "irrelevant" to the expressed needs—even spiritual needs—of our contemporaries; as pastors and as pastoral theologians we are under obligation to maintain the course of this vessel (i.e., the Church catholic), as it has been sailing these same seas of human history, faithfully and in the obedience of graced freedom, for more than two millennia. The pastor must also remember that a focus on the enrichment of graced freedom among members of the *ekklēsia* will ultimately assure that this community of faith will

Conclusion

provide ample evidence of her Christ-like compassion as she endeavors to be ever more faithful in promoting freedom for humanity—freedom from the diversity of ways in which both culture and society entrap souls in serial bondage.

Graced freedom is also and always central to the ministry of pastoral counsel, where the models used in the secular science of psychology can and do provide extremely helpful insights and methodologies to the pastor in his or her role of counsel. It is one area of pastoral ministry in which extensive training is necessary to assure proper care for the welfare of one's congregant, and with few exceptions should only be undertaken by the pastor with the necessary academic and clinical background and expertise. For most clergy the counsel is best centered on the issue of spiritual direction, seeking to help the person gain insight into where he or she is in bondage and the way in which graced freedom can be renewed or revived, through Scripture and prayer, and as the power to escape from bondage. It may well be the case that the form of bondage is a consequence of sin and disobedience—the member himself or herself, or as a victim of another's sinful disobedience—but the awakening to the empowerment of graced freedom can be extremely important to the process of healing and hope for the future. As we have been arguing throughout this essay, graced freedom is freedom for humanity, and the crippling effects of the numerous forms of the soul's (*psyche*) bondage are all too evident to the pastor as he or she tends to his or her people; it is equally clear to the pastor that any soul entrapped in some form of bondage diminishes the victims sense of humanity, and value as one created *imago Dei*. In the image of Christ, pastors are called to set free all who are captive to guilt, shame, and despair of ever being forgiven; and though we cannot do so of our own initiative, we are promised the presence and power of the Holy Spirit who—as the Lord of graced freedom—can and will bring release, renewal, and refreshment to the tortured soul.

Pastoral service takes place within the matrix of four interrelated covenants: (1) the covenant between the pastor and the Lord Christ who called him or her to office, to serve the Lord in serving God's people; (2) the covenant between the pastor and the local church which, with the guidance of the Holy Spirit, called him or her to hold office in a local setting; (3) the covenant between the pastor and the Church catholic, in which he or she vows to uphold, and to pass on in good faith, the traditions of the Christian faith; the covenant between the pastor and his or her colleagues, in which he or she promises a genuine enrichment of the collegiality they share; and

Conclusion

(4) the covenant between the pastor and the ecumenical endeavor, in which he or she commits, in obedience to Christ's prayerful petition, to pursue every avenue for the furtherance of visible unity. Each of the covenants listed entails fulfillment of an aspect of the pastor's ordination vow to be a teacher and preacher of the gospel, furthering the mission and ministry of Christ as he or she is able and according to the gifts of the Spirit he or she possesses. All four forms of pastoral-covenantal relation disclose the centrality of graced freedom in the whole of what the pastor undertakes as he or she sets about serving God in Christ; such freedom is, therefore, evidently freedom for humanity. While it is evident that the pastor must assume tasks of administration, they are only legitimate to the degree that such tasks undertaken are actually representative of ad-ministration (i.e., ministering with) as a shared responsibility shouldered in obedience to the one God being served. This is to define the office of pastor in terms that are better suited to the spiritual realities of the office, rather than co-opting and employing models of leadership and administration from the realm of general business or society. The pastor is only able to carry forward the work with which he or she has been charged with the fullest measure of graced freedom God provides, bearing living witness (i.e., *martyria*) as exemplary to the truth that, as the apostle Paul once asserted: "I am able to do all things through Him who strengthens me" (Phil. 4:13). It is just this "strength" which graced freedom makes possible in the power of the Spirit of Christ Jesus.

What the last sentence of the preceding paragraph implies is that the pastor holding office in the *ekklēsia* is fundamentally accountable for creating an environment suitable to the enlargement of graced freedom, as opposed to spending his or her time experimenting with models of pastoral care and shepherding that have little or no effect on the enrichment of graced freedom. What is vital to the growth of any congregation is always first and foremost the enlargement of graced freedom, and that is to focus all efforts in ministry and mission, primarily, on the health of the heart, mind, spirit, and soul of each individual member and the whole of the *ekklēsia*. Such effort will seek, in all good faith, to promote that form of ministry Paul affirms in his epistle to the Romans (12:1–2): "Therefore, (brethren), by the mercies of God, I urge you to present your bodies as a living sacrifice, holy and pleasing to God; this is your spiritual worship. Do not be conformed to this age, but be transformed by the renewing of your mind, so that you may discern what is the good, pleasing, and perfect will

Conclusion

of God." It is clearly no accident that the apostle ends this exhortation with pointed reference to the "will of God," as only graced freedom enables the believer to that form of obedience and service that will disclose exactly why it is that the "will of God" is "good, pleasing, and perfect." Essentially God's will is "good, pleasing, and perfect," because the will of God is founded on God's eternal love, mercy, forgiveness, and promise. Beyond that, God's will is "good, pleasing, and perfect," because it desires that all of God's children and the whole of creation be set free from bondage to death and decay, in order that, in graced freedom humanity itself can emerge from the darkness of sin's captivity, to breathe in the unsullied air of God's unending affection (i.e., with God, freedom *from* is always freedom *for*).

If any aspect of this essay proves to be controversial, if not contestable, it will be the position taken in this portion of the chapter. We begin with a statement: The embrace of the salvation offered by God in Christ is grounded in the initial and subsequent act of repentance; stated in the words of the apostle Paul: "For godly grief produces a repentance not to be regretted and leading to salvation . . . consider how much diligence this very thing—this grieving as God wills—has produced in you: what a desire to clear yourselves, what indignation, what fear, what deep longing, what zeal, what justice!" (2 Cor. 7:10–11a). We contend that repentance is essential to the sustainability of graced freedom in both the life of the individual believer and in the corporate body of the *ekklēsia*; repentance that recognizes the offense of sin as disobedience and therefore rupture in the relationship with the living God of the covenant ("Against You—and You alone—I have sinned and done what is evil in Your sight" [Ps. 51:4]).

But genuine repentance is also an awareness of those ways in which the rupture in the relationship with God (the vertical level of impact) effects those relationships shared with others (the horizontal level of impact); because "sin" is first a violation and betrayal of God's love, it is also inevitably a violation and betrayal of love for one's brothers and sisters in Christ. There is, perhaps, no clearer sign of the operation of the Holy Spirit in the life of the believer and the *ekklēsia*, than is that which is witnessed in the capacity to repent—or as was often said in select communities of faith—the capacity to welcome the "gift of tears" of remorse for sin. The joy of repentance is in the knowledge that forgiveness comes and there will subsequently be a restoration of graced freedom and the capacity to live in obedience once again. The Christian cannot—and must not try—to escape the reality of what the reformers called the character of *simul justus*

Conclusion

et peccator; this reality of Christian character, for both individual and corporate body, demands a recognition of the centrality of repentance in the life of the Christian and the *ekklēsia*.

So far, not terribly controversial! Now, we would argue that, while the general confession of sin in any or every liturgy has its place in the worship life of the people of God, it has, unfortunately, all too often substituted for the necessity of the individual confessing his or her sins in the ear of another—and in most traditions, where there is respect for the sacramental character of the "confessional," that person would be the pastor or priest. Even in those communities that would define themselves as "evangelical" or even (what we see to be an oxymoron) "independent" such practice of one-on-one confession and repentance of sin should not be seen as all that different from the common practice of, what is normally referred to as, a recommitment to Christ or the traditional "altar call." Our point is simply to state the case, that even in those expressions of Christian worship where "private" confession, or as we have stated the practice, "one-on-one confession and repentance of sin," should not be seen to be all that removed from practices already in effect. Beyond that, one of the aspects of the pastoral office that is in need of reclamation among most Protestant traditions is the pastoral art of "the confessional," in which the pastor hears the sins of another, declares forgiveness, and establishes the ground for the renewal or restoration of graced freedom. Within the relationship of pastoral collegiality, where there is no episcopacy in effect, such confession could be share with a trusted colleague or spiritual director from one's own—or preferably—another Christian confessional body (which would also serve to further the bond of ecumenical relations). More than thirty years in pastoral office have demonstrated the ineffective nature of the common prayer of confession, as employed in the context of the Sunday liturgy, and the necessity for all pastors, regardless of confessional orientation, to now take seriously the necessity for the restoration of "auricular confession" as the primary vehicle for the renewal and restoration of graced freedom as that freedom for humanity, which is at the heart of the gospel and mission to the wider world.

One of the central, if not the most important, responsibilities of the pastor is to officiate the celebration of the sacraments of Baptism and Eucharist (we limit our attention to these two alone only because of their ecumenical significance). As has been stated elsewhere in this essay (see chapter 6), the sacraments represent the liturgical context for both the

Conclusion

conferral and enrichment of graced freedom; the pastor fulfills his or her obligation to the continuance of graced freedom through a proper and respectful celebration of each of the two sacraments. What this "proper and respectful celebration" means is that he or she will not engage in any practice of sacramental celebration that would call the integrity of that same sacrament into question. This will be one of the most crucial tests of the pastor's appreciation for and employment of graced freedom, as such a restriction of celebration of either sacrament will have "political" implications and consequences; there are those who deem both Baptism and participation in the Eucharist as a form of common "right" among those who claim membership in the church/Church, with little or no evident regard for the sacerdotal character of the sacrament and the obligations implicit in their celebration. All too often each of the two sacraments are celebrated with little solemnity and respect as holy things with a holy purpose, treated instead as if Baptism were merely a "rite of passage" for children, and the Eucharist no more than a "common meal of fellowship" within the church/Church; and we can assure the reader, we speak as much from experience, as we do study and observation. What many protestant pastors deny *de jure* (that the sacrament does what it does regardless of the character of the officiant), they practice *de facto*, baptizing the children of those who request this "service" of the church/Church, with little regard for the seriousness of sacramental intent, or commitment to Christ and his *ekklēsia*.

The Eucharist has suffered as well, we contend, but mostly from the unwillingness to enforce the conviction that not all should be welcome at this Altar-Table (which is not the same as affirming the "open table," which is in the interests of ecumenicity), and in particular without the prerequisite confession of sin, repentance, and restoration to a more obedient posture in relation to the Lord and the Lord's expressed will. In our own confessional community (the United Church of Christ), even though the latest worship book and hymnal contain a "Preparatory Service" or "Service of Reconciliation," for the purposes of providing a liturgical setting for such repentance and renewal prior to the celebration of the Eucharist, one surmises that such services are seldom—if ever—employed by most pastors in most local settings of the church/Church. It is not uncommon to find congregations in which the "open table" is extended to everyone—literally!—even those who have no commitment to Christ and the gospel of reconciliation. Even if only anecdotal, most pastors will recognize what is being affirmed here, and join in a wide-ranging *mea culpa*! Yet, as stated in

Conclusion

the previous paragraph, there is the reality of confession, repentance, and restoration to a more faithful practice and celebration of each sacrament, as they represent the otherwise improbable conferral and renewal of graced freedom for individual and *ekklēsia*.[1]

Finally, and in conclusion, it is to be stressed that while this chapter has focused on the responsibilities of the one holding pastoral office, we would be remiss if we concluded our discussion of graced freedom—as freedom for humanity—on that note alone, and in particular in light of the advances that have been made along the ecumenical front, in terms of emphasizing the ministry of the "whole people of God" (what has sometimes been called "the priesthood of all believers"). And so we close with a rather lengthy—yet nonetheless, vital—quote from the document *Baptism, Eucharist and Ministry*:

> The Church is called to proclaim and prefigure the Kingdom of God. It accomplishes this by announcing the Gospel to the world and by its very existence as the body of Christ. In Jesus the Kingdom of God came among us. He offered salvation to sinners. He preached good news to the poor, release to the captives, recovery of sight to the blind, liberation to the oppressed (Luke 4:18). Christ established a new access to the Father. Living in this communion with God, all members of the Church are called to confess their faith and to give account of their hope. They are to identify with the joys and sufferings of all people as they seek to witness in caring love. The members of Christ's body are to struggle with the oppressed towards that freedom and dignity promised with the coming of the Kingdom. This mission needs to be carried out in varying political, social and cultural contexts. In order to fulfill this mission faithfully, they will seek relevant forms of witness and service in each situation. In doing so they bring to the world a foretaste of the joy and glory of God's Kingdom.[2]

---

1. "Solidarity in the eucharistic communion of the body of Christ and responsible care of Christians one another and the world find specific expression in the liturgies: in the mutual forgiveness of sins; the sign of peace; intercession for all; the eating and drinking together; the taking of the elements to the sick and those in prison or the celebration of the eucharist with them. All these manifestations of love in the eucharist are directly related to Christ's own testimony as a servant, in whose servanthood Christians themselves participate. As God in Christ has entered into the human situation, so Eucharistic liturgy is near to the concrete and particular situations of men and women" (*Baptism, Eucharist, and Ministry*, 14).

2. Ibid., 20.

Bibliography

Kittel, Gerhard, and Gerhard Friedrich, eds. *Theological Dictionary of the New Testament: Abridged in One Volume.* Translated by Geoffrey W. Bromiley. Grand Rapids: Eerdmans, 1985.
World Council of Churches. *Baptism, Eucharist and Ministry.* Faith and Order Paper 111. Geneva: WCC, 1982.
World Council of Churches. *Ecumenical Perspectives on Baptism, Eucharist and Ministry.* Faith and Order Paper 116. Geneva: WCC, 1983.

www.ingramcontent.com/pod-product-compliance
Lightning Source LLC
Chambersburg PA
CBHW071858160426
43197CB00013B/2522